WITHDRAWN

UTSA LIBRARIES

P9-DTS-106

FAMILY EXPERIENCES
WITH
MENTAL ILLNESS

RENEWALS 458-4574

	DATE DUE		
GAYLORD			PRINTED IN U.S.A.

WITHDRAWN
UTSA LIBRARIES

FAMILY EXPERIENCES

—— WITH ——

MENTAL ILLNESS

Richard Tessler and Gail Gamache

AUBURN HOUSE
Westport, Connecticut • London

Library
University of Texas
at San Antonio

Library of Congress Cataloging-in-Publication Data

Tessler, Richard C.
  Family experiences with mental illness / Richard Tessler and Gail Gamache.
    p. cm.
  Includes bibliographical references and index.
  ISBN 0–86569–251–3 (alk. paper)—ISBN 0–86569–252–1 (pbk. : alk. paper)
    1. Mentally ill—Family relationships. 2. Mental illness. I. Gamache, Gail,
  1938– II. Title.
  RC455.4.F3 T46 2000
  362.2'0422—dc21   99–045816

British Library Cataloguing in Publication Data is available.

Copyright © 2000 by Richard Tessler and Gail Gamache

All rights reserved. No portion of this book may be
reproduced, by any process or technique, without the
express written consent of the publisher.

Library of Congress Catalog Card Number: 99–045816
ISBN: 0–86569–251–3
      0–86569–252–1 (pbk.)

First published in 2000

Auburn House, 88 Post Road West, Westport, CT 06881
An imprint of Greenwood Publishing Group, Inc.
www.greenwood.com

Printed in the United States of America

The paper used in this book complies with the
Permanent Paper Standard issued by the National
Information Standards Organization (Z39.48–1984).

10 9 8 7 6 5 4 3 2 1

Library
University of Texas
at San Antonio

Dedicated to
families living with mental illness
and to
the late James R. Greenley,
who recognized the wisdom and courage of families
and the lessons to be learned from them.

Contents

Figures and Tables

FIGURES

TABLES

Preface

Although their reactions may vary, virtually all family members experience their relatives' mental illness in life-changing ways. This is true whether it is a widowed mother who provides a home for an adult son with schizophrenia, a retired father who makes financial sacrifices to help his daughter with bipolar disorder pay her rent, a brother who chooses to distance himself emotionally and physically from a brother who is noncompliant with medication, or an adult child who worries about her mother's increasing inability to care for herself. The fact that most of the time, family members are able to adapt to the mental illness of a relative, often in the most supportive of ways, speaks to the resilience of the American family and its capacity to find strength in adversity.

In this book, we use survey research methods to examine how the family experience with mental illness tends to be structured by factors that are external to the disorder per se. Among the factors we examine are family relationships (parent, spouse, son, sister, etc.), living with or apart from the relative with mental illness, the family members' attitudes toward mental illness, and relations with mental health professionals. We also take into account larger changes in the organization and financing of mental health services. By linking social, psychological, and economic factors to the family experience, we attempt to go beyond simple generalizations about the burden of mental illness to explain the substantial variation in how family members perceive, evaluate, and respond to the mental illness of a relative.

All of the relatives with mental illness were, at some point in our studies, involved in the public system of care in Ohio. Many are poor by any American standard, and the same can be said of their families. Like their relatives with mental illness, these family members lack the kinds of social resources that one typically finds among middle-class families, command little power or influence, and are among those least likely to advocate for themselves or their relatives.

The research on which this book is based was conducted over a span of ten years with two different cohorts of patients and families. Directly or indirectly, they all experienced the same public system of care in Ohio. But that system of care was itself evolving. In the late 1980s, it was evolving in response to three grants from the Robert Wood Johnson Foundation designed to reduce fragmentation in state mental health systems by centralizing responsibility for patient care and supporting more residential alternatives. By the mid-1990s, the Ohio Department of Mental Health was changing yet again, this time in response to the emergence of managed care for its Medicaid and Medicare patients. The family experiences we analyze occurred against the backdrop of these two cycles of reform, the first of which we studied during 1989–1992, and the second of which we studied during 1995–1997.

All 13 chapters of this book are original in that none has been previously published. They may be read selectively or in their entirety. However they are read, we hope that the results will be helpful to family members who have relatives with mental illness, while also helping mental health professionals to better understand the family experience and state mental health authorities to design even more responsive services. If the experiences of family members who make up the informal system of care really matter, then their messages surely deserve to be heard.

Curiously, it was not only the system of care that changed as we moved into the 1990s. The terminology for referring to persons with mental illness was also changing. In the late 1980s, it was "politically correct" to refer to patients as clients or consumers, reflecting their relationship to the professional system of care, except in historical discussions of hospitalization, in which the term *patient* seemed more appropriate. Thus, Part I, which reviews the history of family research, includes some references to patients, and Part II of this book, which covers the era of the RWJ initiative, is replete with references to clients and consumers. By the mid-1990s, it had become "politically correct" to refer to persons with mental illness in ways that emphasized their connections to families. Thus, in Part III, we refer to them mainly as relatives with mental illness. Rather than standardize terminology across the different sections of the book, we have chosen to go with the times and the shifting sands of political correctness.

Acknowledgments

John Harney planted the seed for this book that took root and grew into the product that you, the reader, now hold in your hand. Many others supported and nurtured the project along the way. We thank Howard Goldman and Anthony Lehman of the University of Maryland Medical School, Jan Greenberg and the late James Greenley of the University of Wisconsin, Allan Horwitz and David Mechanic of Rutgers University, Mark Tausig of the University of Akron, David Biegel of Case Western Reserve University, and Aart Schene of the University of Amsterdam. We also benefited from interaction with senior researchers from the National Alliance for the Mentally Ill (NAMI). From NAMI we thank Victoria Conn, Agnes Hatfield, and Harriet Lefley.

We could not have written the book without the grants that supported both the research and the writing. The longitudinal data collections were supported by grants from the National Institute of Mental Health (NIMH Grant No. R01MH44683), and the Ohio Department of Mental Health, Office of Program Evaluation and Research (ODMH Grant Nos. 1087 and 1122). From NIMH we thank Thomas Lalley and Charles Windle, and from ODMH we thank Dee Roth and her project associates, Gail Burns and Dushka Crane-Ross. Most of the data were collected under contract with the Institute for Survey Research (ISR) associated with Temple University. From ISR, we thank Ann Shinefeld and Ellin Spector. Preparation of the manuscript was supported by a grant from the Robert Wood Johnson Foundation (Grant No. 23335). From the foundation, we thank our project officer, Margery Gutman. The final editing of the manuscript took place while we were both on interagency personnel assignments (IPAs) at the Connecticut/Massachusetts VA Mental Illness Research, Education and Clinical Center (MIRECC). From the MIRECC, we thank Robert Rosenheck for helping us to include the most recent findings in family burden research with veteran populations.

We benefited greatly from interactions with colleagues at the University of Massachusetts. In the mid-1980s, the first author worked with Gayle Gubman and Lewis Killian to develop a theory of stages in family response to mental illness, and in the late 1980s with Gene Fisher to develop measures of family burden and to launch the research presented in Part II. Throughout the many years of our research on family burden, the Social & Demographic Research Institute (SADRI) under the leadership of Peter H. Rossi and Douglas Anderson has been the most supportive of environments. From SADRI, we thank Dee Weber, who managed our databases, and Karen Mason, who proofread the entire manuscript and constructed the index.

We want to extend a personal thank-you to the many family members in Ohio who participated in our surveys, and who shared their attitudes and experiences with us. We are proud to be your spokespersons. Finally, we want to publicly thank our own family members, our spouses—Hugh Gamache and Patricia Gorman; our children—Gail Fisher, Melissa Gamache, Timothy Gamache, Carol Gamache-Taylor, Catherine Regish, Hannah Tessler, and Zoe Tessler; and our grandchildren—Christopher Fisher, Heather Taylor, Anthony Gamache, Lindsay Regish, Benjamin Gamache, Michael Regish, Constance Bosinger, and Lauren Gamache.

Before his death in 1996, James Greenley agreed to review the manuscript and write a foreword to it. Had he lived to accomplish that task, he surely would have had much to say that would have led to improvements in the final manuscript. For the parts of the book that remain imperfect without his counsel, we accept full responsibility. May the parts that are insightful and compassionate honor his memory.

Acronyms

FBIS	Family Burden Interview Schedule
FM	Family Member
FY	Fiscal Year
HCFA	Health Care Financing Administration
HUD	Housing and Urban Development
IPA	Interagency Personnel Assignment
ISR	Institute for Survey Research
LCO	Longitudinal Study of Mental Health Services and Consumer Outcomes in a Changing System
MHIS	Mental Health Information System
MIRECC	Mental Illness Research, Education and Clinical Center
NAMI	National Alliance for the Mentally Ill
NIMH	National Institute of Mental Health
ODMH	Ohio Department of Mental Health
OhioCare	Statewide plan for mandatory enrollment of Medicaid beneficiaries in a managed health care system
PACT	Program of Assertive Community Treatment

RMI	Relative with Mental Illness
RWJ Foundation	Robert Wood Johnson Foundation
SADRI	Social & Demographic Research Institute
SSDI	Social Security Disability Insurance
SSI	Supplemental Security Income
T1	Time 1
T2	Time 2
T3	Time 3

PART I

Introduction

Chapter 1

Mental Illness and the Family

In an earlier era, persons with severe mental illness would have been hospitalized, perhaps for life, and their family members would have been blamed as the cause of the illness. Since the 1950s and beyond, when changes in mental health policy located care in the community and new biological explanations for mental illness became salient, family members have faced the dilemma of choosing whether (and in what ways) to be involved when a relative with mental illness lives mainly in the community. Although modern (and postmodern) families can and do extend themselves to help out at times of acute crisis, the indication is that families experience more difficulty in the face of long-term problems and enduring disabilities. These "private troubles" find their institutional expression in dilemmas about the caregiving role of the family in American society and the limits of its responsibilities. Family members find their generosity tested, requiring them to examine the costs and benefits of their involvement (Gubman and Tessler 1987). How family members resolve such dilemmas is the focus of this book.

The National Institute of Mental Health estimated that at any point in time, between 617,400 and 764,400 adults in the United States have diagnosable mental disorders serious enough to interfere with the normal life course of employment, marriage, and adult autonomy (Kemp 1994). The family members about whom we write in this book have relatives who fall within this category of serious mental illness, with most suffering from schizophrenia and severe affective disorders. It is difficult to estimate precisely the numbers of family members who are affected, but if we assume the presence of at least one close family member per diagnosed person, it is likely that they number well over a million and a half.

Almost 50 years ago, sociologists Talcott Parsons and Renee Fox noted the tendency of the American urban family to relinquish responsibility for caring for the sick to professionals (1952). They linked this social change to particular vulnerabilities of the modern American family, including its small size, tendency toward isolation and segregation from other social institutions, emotional intensity and high level of affective demands, individualism, and independence. As they stated about the family, "pressures from the demands of the sick strike it at what appears to be a vulnerable point" (p. 36).

Although Parsons and Fox did not specifically develop the case of mental illness, they were explicit in acknowledging that the liabilities of family care also extend to that arena. Parsons and Fox did not envision the trend toward deinstitutionalization; that is, of course, what occurred in the mental health field only a few years after the publication of their classic article. Increasingly, psychiatric patients and their families learned that the primary locus of care was to be the community, and not the hospital. For families this meant that the trend toward relinquishing responsibility for patient care to specialized professionals and institutions was being turned back onto them, at the same time that the modern nuclear family was being replaced by the postmodern family with its less rigid obligations and expectations with respect to caring for ill members.

This was especially burdensome when residential and community mental health resources were not well developed or where the patient was reluctant to make use of them. In the ensuing years, families were faced with the presence of relatives with mental illness living in the community, and with needs for care and supervision requiring them to make personal decisions about the limits of their involvement (Fisher, Benson, and Tessler 1990).

One response of family members was to point out that responsibility for care was being transferred from the institution to *them*. A founding member of an advocacy group, the National Alliance for the Mentally Ill (NAMI), suggested that mental health professionals should have asked, "How well are families able to manage caregiving on a 24-hour basis that was once done by a staff on three 8-hour shifts?" (Hatfield 1983). The term *family burden* has come "to characterize the load, carrying capacity, and strain experienced by family members" as they attempted to replace those three 8-hour shifts in the absence of community services (Gubman and Tessler 1987). In the discussion that follows, our use of the term *family burden* refers only to the burden of mental illness on the family, and not to the person with mental illness as the burden.

We need also to remember that people with mental illness are family members, too, that is, sons and daughters, brothers and sisters, and nephews and nieces. Until recently, persons with mental illness were always categorized as patients, a status that implies their relationships to treatment professionals, and in so doing their family relationships were downplayed. With the rise of the consumer movement and new sensitivity to labeling, consumers of mental health services have been active in putting people first. We no longer refer without thinking to "the mentally ill" but to people with mental illness.

This book focuses on dilemmas of kinship to emphasize the difficult choices that confront family members when faced with the mental illness of an adult relative that is serious and persistent. Throughout this book, a range of difficult choices that face family members will be described, and results from two family studies (described in Chapters 2 and 9) will be used to illustrate how family members respond. Family members are not homogeneous in their recognition, evaluation, or response to mental illness. As we will show, family members resolve their dilemmas in a variety of ways.

To a great extent the dilemmas that arise for family members are the result of changing policies toward persons with mental illness. As noted above, social policies toward persons with mental illness in the last three decades mandate an increasing emphasis on community care. The deinstitutionalization movement brought age-old responsibilities back to family members, who saw themselves after 100 years of institutionalization confronted with new obligations toward their ill or handicapped members. The current policy may also be referred to as noninstitutionalization, since many clients have never had a long-term hospitalization.

Although professionals are responsible for managing the *formal system* of mental health care for persons with severe mental illness, it is family members who represent the informal system of care. When care is based in the community, the informal system is likely to be as important to the consumer as the formal system. In an era in which institutions have declined, and formal supports in the community are lacking, community care often spells family involvement (Hatfield 1983).

Ironically, at the same time that current mental health policies encourage community living, the postmodern family, which differs from the modern nuclear family that Parsons and Fox described, is also rarely prepared for giving long-term care to an ill family member. According to Tausig, Michello, and Subedi, "The nuclear family provided clear-cut, often rigid rules of behavior and expectations. . . . The new postmodern family is more flexible, but more vulnerable to pressures from outside" (1999, 61).

Most of us are not prepared nor do we expect to have to order our lives to the rhythm of another person's serious illness. Nonetheless, some family members accept the caregiving role with a great sense of familial obligation, perhaps believing that the family is providing the only real care available. They advocate for their relatives, provide shelter, assist in the activities of daily living, and supervise troublesome behaviors, while also providing emotional support and encouragement.

Other family members when faced with long-term illness prefer that their relative obtain as much independence as is feasible, and look to the professional system of care to make this possible. This does not mean that such family members wish to be uninvolved, but rather to be as involved as one would be with any other family member. Such families will come to the rescue as the safety net of last resort, stepping in only when independent housing and vocational solutions fail or when income maintenance programs are cut back. But the commitment of these families is more limited and is meant to be short-term. In those instances in which levels of burden have become unbearable, and the limits of generosity reached, some family members choose to disengage from the consumer (Tessler et al. 1992). Kinship obligations are strong but not indestructible.

Family members have faced the dilemma of whether and how to support a relative with mental illness since deinstitutionalization, but until recently they have been largely absent in public policy debates. One response has been the formation of organized family groups, particularly the National Alliance for the Mentally Ill (Mechanic 1994). The family movement has been one of the most important developments in this field, growing from modest beginnings in 1978 to more than 1,000 chapters today. The rise of the family movement has helped family members grapple with the stigma of mental illness through sharing experiences with one another, and by speaking collectively in protest when media presentations are stereotyping. Many family members have found a measure of empowerment through self-help and advocacy groups, which provide information about psychiatric disorders, encourage adaptive coping strategies, offer support and mutual help, and seek to have their voices heard by legislators (Norton, Wandersman, and Goldman 1993).

The return of persons with mental illness to the community has also caused many professionals to rethink their beliefs about the causes of mental illness, to desist from blaming family members, and instead to look to families as partners in caregiving. The new respect being garnered by organized family groups is in marked contrast to the attitudes of an earlier era, when parents and particularly mothers were routinely blamed for causing the disorder and excluded from treatment decisions. In this area there have been recent improvements between family members and mental health professionals (Tessler et al. 1992).

In the past, the focus of research was on the impact of the family on the person with mental illness (Fisher, Benson, and Tessler 1990). The impact of the person with mental illness on the family was until the mid-1980s a relatively neglected area of evaluation research. Researchers, excepting those associated with organized family groups, were failing to include the experiences of families when evaluating mental health services for the consumer. Much has changed since the mid-1980s, and family impact has now become an important area of research, with many instruments in existence, and an accumulating body of knowledge about family caregiving (Schene, Tessler, and Gamache 1994).

Recent studies of novel medications such as clozapine are now using measures of family burden as part of the assessment of drug effectiveness, and an innovative cost-effectiveness study in the *New England Journal of Medicine* included days lost from work by family members as one of the costs of mental illness (Rosenheck et al. 1997). Although a major Virginia study of clozapine clearly showed that as patients improve (and especially as their social functioning improves) family burden declines, the improvement with clozapine was not great enough to result in a significant decline in family burden (R. Rosenheck, personal communication). Family issues, however, are now part of mainstream evaluation research.

STAGES IN FAMILY RESPONSE

How family members respond to the mental illness of a relative under the current policy, what roles they choose, and how these roles change over the life cycle of both consumer and family, have far-reaching implications for community-based long-term care.

Responses can be described in terms of stages, although the process of adaptation varies from family to family (Tessler, Killian, and Gubman 1987). Perhaps the first dilemma that family members face is what meaning to assign to the early signs and symptoms of mental illness when they become aware that something is wrong. In the beginning phase of the illness, family members will be uncertain about the diagnosis, and may at first choose to deny that mental illness is involved. One way to resolve this dilemma is to accept the medical labeling of the problem as one that requires intervention from outside the family. When this occurs, it is usually family members who get the relative to professional help. In this stage, family members typically have great faith in mental health professionals, and are hopeful that a cure can be found.

As crises reoccur, another dilemma emerges for family members when there develops a grim recognition that cures are neither quick nor certain. Without a cure, their relative with serious and persistent mental illness will certainly require ongoing care to be sustained in the community. Some families gain relief during this period through insisting that the consumer lead as normal a life as possible by establishing an independent residence.

The recognition of chronicity is often followed by a loss of faith in mental health professionals, or at least a lessening of confidence in them. With the loss of confidence in professionals comes a belief in the family's own expertise, which is based on experience dealing with recurrent crises. However, even under the best of circumstances, families tend to worry about the future and what will happen to their relative when they are no longer there to help. In extreme cases, family members may live with uncertainty because they have lost all contact and do not know where their relative with mental illness can be found.

Stoneall (1983) observed that deinstitutionalized persons and their families may oscillate between periods of closeness and periods of separation. Although family roles include some obligation to give help, separation tends to occur when the person with mental illness rejects the demands and conditions of support imposed by family members. Separation may also occur when family members can no longer tolerate their relative's failure to comply with these demands. Stoneall has likened these relationships to an accordion, in that both come together, move apart, and then may come together again.

THE DIMENSIONS OF BURDEN

Severe mental disorders such as schizophrenia, bipolar disorder, and major depression may represent obstacles to independent living and life satisfaction for those who suffer from them. Employment opportunities may be reduced, self-care may be impeded, and the capacity for social relationships may be severely diminished. When treatment is outside of the institution, a critical issue for persons with mental illness is where to live. Probably as many as a third of consumers live with their families, some with spouses but many others in their parents' home at a time when most in their age cohort have left the family home to live independently (Tessler and Goldman 1982; Fisher et al. 1992). When a family takes on the dual role of housing provider and primary caregiver, the potential burden may be very large indeed.

The consequences of being related to someone suffering from severe mental illness can be roughly divided into the obligation to offer long-term extensive *care* and the emotional *distress* and *worries* related to the consumer. The former requires close contact between consumer and family member, whereas the latter may also exist when kinship ties have unraveled or the amount of contact is very small. Researchers have described this distinction as caring *for* and caring *about* (Graham 1983).

Without the psychiatric hospital to provide for basic needs, persons with mental illness must rely on themselves or the formal or informal systems of care. A major dilemma for family members is whether and in what ways to become involved in helping the person with mental illness to meet these basic needs. Family members who choose to be involved may give a great deal of assistance with activities of daily living, such as providing personal care, preparing meals, doing household chores and laundry, shopping, and helping with transportation.

Some family members also have to learn to cope with delusions, hallucinations, attention seeking, stealing, inappropriate sexual behavior, unreasonable demands, verbal abuse, disturbances during the night, behaviors that are threatening or violent, talk or threats of suicide, and alcohol or drug abuse. Coping with these symptoms and behaviors often requires lengthy, complex, and distressing negotiations (Lefley 1987a). Although rare, there are reported cases of injuries resulting from physical abuse by the consumer (Straznickas, McNiel, and Binder 1993; Estroff et al. 1994).

If the onset of mental illness comes after attaining gainful employment, there may be financial consequences when the relative with mental illness is not able to work at all or when he or she works fewer hours because of the illness. Caregiving may also force family members to work less or to give up their jobs. Ironically, both events may occur along with a rise in expenses related to psychiatric or health care, and medication (Franks 1990). Other economic repercussions may flow from the consumer's inability to manage money, or as a result of destructive behavior.

Caring for or about a relative with mental illness may also have consequences for the mental health of the family members involved. Some family members experience a sense of loss with accompanying grief, comparable to the process of bereavement (Miller et al. 1990). A variety of other negative emotions have been reported that are thought to result from the stress of long-term caregiving, as well as the nature and stigma of mental illness.

Caring for and caring about are not necessarily linked. When a family member refuses to take on the role of *caring for* the consumer, he or she may nevertheless *care deeply about* the consumer. By the same token, caring for does not necessarily imply caring about. Just as the personality of the relative suffering from mental illness may change, so may the relationship with that person. In the absence of reciprocity, the process of caregiving may itself endanger the relationship. Thus, another difficulty lies in keeping alive warm feelings when caregiving becomes burdensome.

Mental illness has an impact on marital relationships (Clausen and Yarrow 1955). When reciprocal relationships are disrupted by illness, one spouse may be forced to take on a greater proportion of formerly shared tasks. As a consequence, the interpersonal relationships between the spouses can become strained. Disruption of the marital relationship is often followed by separation and divorce. When the consumer is also a parent, it may be necessary for other family members to help in caring for his or her minor children. Parenting by persons with mental illness has, unfortunately, been neglected in the family burden literature (Gamache, Tessler and Nicholson 1995).

Studies of the impact on family have paid little attention to the burden carried by family members when the client lives elsewhere. (For an exception see Carpentier et al. 1992.) Even when the client lives independently, family members may still be involved, and some may expend a great deal of time and effort in providing assistance and support. Family members may also experience the psychological costs of having a relative with a serious mental illness without sharing the same home. Thus, it is important to assess the burden of these families and compare it with the burden experienced by family members when the client is living with them (Gubman and Tessler 1987).

THE OFF-TIMEDNESS OF CAREGIVING

One reason that caregiving presents a dilemma is that the care provided is neither age-appropriate nor culturally expected. In modern industrialized societies, *adults* are expected to be independent of their family of origin and to care for themselves from the moment they end their formal education unless they are disabled by illness. Caregiving is a relatively modern concept that has come to describe the relationship that exists between *adults* who are related through kinship. In addition to the family relationships that already exist (e.g., mother and adult son), the onset of mental illness adds the new roles of caregiver and care recipient. The caregiver assumes an unpaid and unanticipated responsibility for another adult, and the care recipient is typically disabled and unable to achieve adult autonomy or to fulfill the reciprocal obligations associated with normal adult relationships.

Thus, care becomes caregiving when it is out of synchrony with the appropriate stage in the life cycle. Caregivers are bound by kinship obligations that go beyond those normally associated with a family role at a particular stage. The onset of a severe mental illness affects all family members. However, in virtually all societies, caregivers are disproportionately female (Cook 1988; Ascher-Svanum and Sobel 1989).

Providing assistance to a relative with mental illness may affect all aspects of one's life, from daily routines to changes in lifestyle. Personal relationships outside the household may be affected adversely by having less time for social activities because of caregiving, and by stigma—leading to attempts to conceal the mental illness. Both time constraints and stigma tend to limit the amount of social contact outside the family and can result in a profound sense of isolation (Lefley 1989).

POSITIVE ASPECTS OF CAREGIVING

Burden research by definition focuses on the negative aspects of the family experience (Schene, Tessler, and Gamache 1994, 1996). As our discussion of the nature of burden has shown, caregiver burden refers to a broad range of difficulties experienced by family members. Although the literature has given less attention to the positive aspects of the family experience, caring for or caring about a relative with mental illness may also bring special rewards to some family members. Caregivers may enjoy the company of the family member, feel he or she is an important part of their life, and feel pride and experience happiness as a result of their continuing relationship. A balanced view of the family experience requires looking at these more positive aspects of caregiving.

Caregivers potentially derive a variety of instrumental and affective benefits, and some family members may believe that the experience has contributed to their personal growth. In one study, parents reported more gratifications than burdens when caring for adult sons and daughters with schizophrenia (Bulger, Wandersman, and Goldman 1993). To the extent that consumers can contribute to the functioning of the household, or fulfill other supportive familial obligations, the costs to the family may be partially offset. Another recent study in rural Wisconsin has reported that the instrumental and expressive contributions of adult persons with serious mental illness to their families are substantial. Between 50 and 80 percent of the clients in this survey contributed to their families (Greenberg, Greenley, and Benedict 1994).

The client may also benefit. As early as 1974, Kreisman and Joy noted that "when the patient contributed to the household rather than taxed its limited resources, there was significantly greater likelihood that the patient would remain out of the hospital" (p. 48).

THE RESEARCH

In this book we present the results from two longitudinal studies of family members of persons with mental illness in Ohio. The research presented in the following chapters is based on interviews with two distinct sets of family members from two different studies in Ohio. The first was a study of family members whose relatives were the intended beneficiaries of a major initiative by the Robert Wood Johnson Foundation (RWJ Foundation) to improve the mental health system. The second was a study of family members whose relatives were clients of the Ohio Department of Mental Health (ODMH) during an era of change to managed care. Detailed descriptions of the studies, the two family member/consumer samples, and summaries of previously published materials are provided in Chapters 2 and 9.

The aims of each study varied somewhat according to the contemporary policy interest in family members at the time of the data collections. The main goal of the RWJ family study was to examine family experiences with mental illness with respect to family burden, residence, and continuity of care. The main goal of the ODMH family study was to examine family experiences with mental illness with respect to family member evaluations of mental health professionals, services, and systems.

In what follows, we will look at the commonalities of family experiences (of which there are many) as well as the differences. Typically our inquiries will draw on quantitative methods, but where appropriate we also include vignettes and quotations from family members. Although some of the details have been changed to preserve confidentiality, we have tried to preserve the essence of these family experiences.

Depending on the stage of the family life cycle, caregivers in both studies held the family roles of *parents* caring for adult children, *adult children* caring for a parent, a *well spouse* caring for an ill spouse, or a *sibling* caring for a disabled brother or sister. Also involved were *secondary kin*, including grandmothers and aunts and other kinlike relations. Family experiences with mental illness are not the same either within or between families. As we will see from the research, one's role in the family hierarchy, and whether the family member (FM) and the relative with mental illness (RMI) were living together or apart, each influenced and helped to structure the family experience.

The research presented in Part II was occasioned by the major initiative of the Robert Wood Johnson Foundation in the 1980s to improve patient outcomes by centralizing responsibility for providing long-term mental health services, and by expanding supportive housing options. Throughout Part II, we will analyze family experiences during the period in which the RWJ program was implemented.

In the mid-1990s, we revisited the research landscape, finding that both the system of care and the issues for research had evolved from what we had understood them to be only three to five years earlier. Although burden remained a concern, it was not the dominant concern that it had been in the 1980s, as family members (among others) had broadened their agenda to include other issues in mental health and social policy (Mechanic 1999). These emerging issues—managed care, parity, and the limits of family responsibility—as well as the research that was designed to addressed them, will be taken up in Part III. Part IV consists of a single concluding chapter in which the vexing dilemmas of kinship are summarized and the implications of the research discussed.

PART II

Family Experiences in Ohio: 1989–1992

Chapter 2

The Research Landscape

The RWJ Foundation's Program for the Chronically Mentally Ill, launched in 1986, was planned as a services demonstration with the goal of helping "the chronically mentally ill function more effectively in their daily lives" (Goldman, Morrissey, and Ridgely 1994, 39). A total of $29 million was provided to nine demonstration sites (Austin, Texas; Baltimore, Maryland; Charlotte, North Carolina; Cincinnati, Columbus, and Toledo, Ohio; Denver, Colorado; Honolulu, Hawaii; and Philadelphia, Pennsylvania). The funds were to be used by each site to create a centralized mental health authority or to enhance an existing one. According to the program logic, centralizing all aspects of "administrative, fiscal, and clinical responsibility for individuals with chronic mental illness . . . would expand resources and services, and such services would improve continuity of care and quality of life" (p. 39). Case management and housing options were to be particular focuses (also see Aiken, Sommers, and Cohen 1986; Shore and Cohen 1990).

THE FAMILY STUDY

A family component was not an integral part of the original design of the national evaluation of the RWJ Foundation program. Rather, the evaluation was designed to focus on system and client outcomes.

However, the need to include family outcomes was apparent from the *logic model*, which alluded to expected benefits for families flowing from improvements in the mental health system (Goldman et al. 1990).

In the winter of 1988, researchers at the University of Massachusetts at Amherst developed a proposal to examine two issues related to family burden that had not yet been adequately examined in the literature. One issue was the extent to which burden is increased when the member with mental illness lives with the family, or conversely, the extent to which relocation to other residential settings reduces family burden. The second issue concerned the extent to which the provision of care in a coordinated, continuous, and timely manner benefited the family as well as the member with mental illness. The resulting proposal, titled "Continuity of Care, Residence, and Family Burden" (Richard Tessler, principal investigator and Gene Fisher, co-principal investigator), was submitted to the National Institute of Mental Health in February 1988, reviewed twice, and funded in 1989.

To make the best use of resources, we chose to conduct the family study in Columbus, Cincinnati, and Toledo, Ohio, where client interviewing was also planned. The three sites represented a subgroup of the nine American cities chosen as RWJ Foundation grantees. We chose to focus on the Ohio sites because the presence of a single state mental health authority increased homogeneity between sites and centralized the data collection effort. The Ohio Department of Mental Health was a leader in mental health reform through its support of county mental health boards and its shared governance approach.

In Ohio, responsibility for persons with mental illness is vested in a series of county- or multi-county-based boards that have broad representation appointed both locally and by the State Department of Mental Health and are given the responsibility to plan and administer all programs for the mentally ill in the jurisdiction. These boards provide no services directly, but contract for them, combining resources from state grants and contracts as well as revenues generated by millage (a local tax levy that supplies resources for the care and treatment of persons with mental illness and retardation in the jurisdiction). The RWJ Foundation initiative was expected to enhance the boards' ability to function as centralized authorities for services to persons with severe mental illness.

All three sites developed housing plans that included proposals for how they would use foundation funds and distribute HUD Section 8 certificates. Other efforts to enrich housing options for the target population were also pursued. A variety of service innovations reflecting the specific gaps and needs of the geographic area were implemented.

SPECIFIC AIMS

From the beginning, it was clear that among its objectives, the RWJ Foundation intended families to be beneficiaries of an improved service delivery system. Changes in the organization, financing, and delivery of client services were reasoned to affect family members indirectly by increasing the clients' residential independence and continuity of care. When there exists an involved family member, a plausible hypothesis is that if the client is receiving services that are consecutive and related to one another, the carrying load of particular family members will be reduced. Although it had a long history in general medicine, continuity of care was a relatively new concept in mental health (Steinwachs 1979; Rogers and Curtis 1980; Tessler, Willis, and Gubman 1986). Our approach was to define continuity of care in terms of the provision of continuous case management services designed to help the client plan and get needed services such as therapy, medication, work or employment, and housing. The strategy for research was to link family data with client data to examine whether and in what ways the system changes had an impact on families. The original design called for linking family and client data with case manager data, but the significant numbers of case managers who did not return the self-administered questionnaire obviated this part of the design.

Working contractually with the Institute for Survey Research in Philadelphia (Ellin Spector, project director), we began to collect family burden data in 1989. The research plan called for linking family burden data with continuity of care data to be collected concurrently by a team of researchers from the University of Maryland Medical School (Howard Goldman, principal investigator). Burden was assessed in face-to-face interviews with multiple family members, and then reassessed at two 12-month intervals using telephone interviews. Thus, the data used in the analyses and discussions presented in the following chapters come from two separate but related research efforts. As this chapter will show, the vagaries of funding cycles made it impossible to synchronize the client and family interviews, but the linking of the two independent sources of data was useful nonetheless.

MEASUREMENT APPROACHES

The first task was to develop an interview schedule, which we called the Family Burden Interview Schedule (FBIS). The FBIS had its origins in a baseline questionnaire developed for an impact evaluation of the Massachusetts Family Support Program in 1987. Services designed specifically for family members were expected to reduce negative aspects of the family experience. The questionnaire included various dimensions of objective burden associated with caregiving and an attitude toward professionals scale. A follow-up survey of family members was designed to be administered by telephone to 156 family members. Rigorous psychometric analyses were applied to these items (Fisher 1988). The results of the impact evaluation indicated that reductions in caregiving were associated with education programs and respite (Fisher 1989; Benson et al. 1996).

An expanded and revised protocol was pretested in a structured interview format using a sample of National Alliance for the Mentally Ill members in Philadelphia. The version arising from the pretest experience was then used in the family component of the RWJ Foundation evaluation. The measures presented in the following chapters are based on the psychometric analyses conducted using longitudinal data from the Ohio study.

Recall that one of the specific aims was to link family burden with services to the client to examine changes related to the RWJ Foundation's program. We strove to incorporate mental health services into the research design in two ways. The first was in the family interviews, where we included a module on family member contacts with mental health professionals, reasons for the contact, satisfaction, and attitudes toward mental health professionals in general. The results from the baseline interviews incorporating this module have been reported elsewhere (Tessler, Gamache, and Fisher 1991).

The other approach to the measurement of services was to derive information about client service utilization from the client interview and to link it with the family burden data. This has some methodological advantages since the two sources of data are independent of each other, and the family impact of the clients' use of services can be evaluated even if the family is unaware of the clients' patterns of use. The fact that the clients were interviewed three times also makes it possible to measure continuity of care, which was an important part of the program logic. We hoped to test the hypothesis that less family burden would be associated with the clients receiving continuity of care, and to examine this hypothesis under different conditions of client residence.

TIMELINE

Both the clients and the family members were interviewed at three points in time. At the baseline interview (Time 1, hereafter T1), the vast majority of the interviews were done in person at the home of the family member. Some exceptions led us to conduct the interview by phone, such as when the respondent lived more than 50 miles away, or when the respondent did not want the interviewer to come to the house. At Time 2 (T2) and Time 3 (T3), separated by one year, we mainly did telephone interviews to reduce costs, except in a small number of cases where personal interviews were necessary to convert refusals.

The family study titled "Continuity of Care, Residence, and Family Burden" spanned two years in the life of the RWJ Foundation initiative and drew on data elements from the client study. Figure 2.1 illustrates the timing of the family and client interviews. The top line shows the period during which the University of Maryland interviewed the clients shortly after their discharge from a 24-hour inpatient facility. The bottom line reveals the problem in synchrony between the two sets of interviews. The third client interview is most contemporary with the measures of the first family member interview. It is obvious that we could use client measures of continuity of care only with baseline family burden measures. Thus, all analyses using continuity of care had to use baseline family data. However, a variety of other issues could be addressed across the three waves, including whether or not burden decreased or increased. The analyses presented in this book focus on the 305 family members who were interviewed all three times.

SAMPLE

This section describes the client and family samples. The family sample differed from many prior studies of family members of rela-

Figure 2.1
Time Line of Client and Family Member Data Collections

```
1988            1989            1990            1991            1992

                CLIENT
                0--0---------0--------
                C₁ C₂        C₃
                                FAMILY
                        0-----------0-----------0------
                        F₁          F₂          F₃
                        f=409       f=354       f=305
                        c=204       c=192       c=175
                        time 1      time 2      time 3
```

Notes: C = Client Interview
   F = Family Interview
   f = number of family members interviewed
   c = number of consumers associated with family interviews

tives with severe mental illness that had focused on the family of origin. Until recently, most family studies were based upon samples of white middle-class parents (for exceptions, see Crotty and Kulys, 1986; Pickett et al. 1993; Biegel et al. 1994). Our family members represented a greater variety of kinship and non-kinship ties, and had less formal education and lower income. In addition, the sample was almost equally divided between blacks and whites. Despite the lower-than-expected proportion of co-residence, the sample tended to over-represent families that were currently involved with their relatives with mental illness. It also tended to underrepresent the families of those patients who were perhaps the most troublesome. Consumers who were in trouble with the law, were primarily substance abusers, or who were not legally competent were excluded from the study. In addition, patients and families with greater resources who were able to utilize private services may be underrepresented because the hospitalized patient sample was drawn from the Ohio *state* system of care.

SAMPLE SELECTION AND ATTRITION

Human subjects concerns mandated that clients be asked to name and give permission to interview their family members, and thus we begin by describing clients. Criteria for inclusion in the client study were: length of index stay in a 24-hour mental health setting of less than 120 days; age between 18 and 64; a primary diagnosis of mental illness other than substance abuse; had to meet Ohio standards of disability, including diagnosis, hospitalization, and functional status; could *not* be a forensic client; and had to be English speaking and legally competent. These criteria resulted in a total of 283 clients from Cincinnati, Columbus, and Toledo, Ohio, being identified in 1988 in state hospitals or 24-hour crisis care facilities and interviewed shortly after discharge. At the end of the interview, clients were asked to name up to four members of their immediate family. If fewer than four were volunteered (which occurred in most cases), they were asked to name other relatives or particularly close friends who were "like family" and involved in their daily lives. Seven percent said they had no living relatives or close friends, and were therefore excluded. Approximately 10 percent refused to grant permission to interview any family or close friends. The remaining 234 patients named a total of 564 persons, of whom 517 were deemed eligible for our study. Of those, a total of 409, named by 204 patients, were actually interviewed at baseline.

The 79 patients who did not participate in the study were not statistically different from the 204 patients who had family members interviewed with respect to sex, education, psychiatric symptoms, and need for care. However, nonparticipants were older (mean age = 38 versus 34) and somewhat more likely to be white (58% versus 47%). With respect to living arrangements prior to entering the hospital, they were less likely to be married or living with a significant other (6% versus 18%) and less likely to be living with a family member prior to entering the hospital (22% versus 47%), and more likely to have been homeless at least one night in the past year (33% versus 20%). Rather tellingly, fewer than a third of the nonparticipants (29%) reported that they could turn to their family for help, while more than two-thirds (68%) of the participants said that they could. A probit analysis showed that the client's lack of faith that his or her family would help out in times of need was the dominant predictor of *non*participant status. In short, the family sample tended to over-represent families that are currently involved with and supportive of their relatives with mental illness.

THE RELATIVES WITH MENTAL ILLNESS

Table 2.1 reports the descriptive statistics for the clients. There were slightly more males (53%) than females, and whites (53%)

Table 2.1
Client Characteristics by City

Variable	Total (N = 175)	Cincinnati (n = 85)	Columbus (n = 60)	Toledo (n = 30)	Significance Level
Race (% black)	47.4	57.7	31.7	50.0	p = .008
Sex (% female)	46.9	43.5	53.3	43.3	NS
Age (years)	35.5	36.6	33.6	36.1	NS
Education (years)	11.5	11.4	11.7	11.5	NS
Never Married (%)	52.0	54.1	51.7	46.7	NS
Has Children (% yes)	57.7	55.3	56.7	66.7	NS
Schizophrenia (% yes)	62.1	69.4	45.5	72.4	p = .008

than blacks in the client sample. The average client was 35.5 years old, and had 11.5 years of education. Fifty-two percent had never been married, although 58 percent had children.

A majority (62%) of the clients were diagnosed with schizophrenia with slightly more than a fourth receiving a diagnosis of either bipolar disorder or major depression. Clients had been ill for an average of 14 years, and first received help for mental health problems on average at the age of 22. They averaged a 30-day length of stay in a 24-hour setting prior to participation in the client study. Approximately 43 percent reported that they had had a case manager or helping team during the 12 months preceding the first family interview.

THE FAMILY MEMBERS

Criteria for the family sample included not being a minor (under 18), not being a consumer of mental health services, and not being a treatment professional. A total of 409 family interviews were conducted between October 1989 and March 1990 (T1). A second wave (T2) of interviews took place between October 1990 and March 1991. Three hundred fifty-four family members (associated with 192 clients) were reinterviewed. A third wave was conducted between October 1991 and March 1992, when a total of 305 relatives (linked to 175 clients) were interviewed for the third and final time (T3). The 305 family members who completed all three interviews are the basis for the analyses presented throughout this book.

Table 2.2
Family Member Characteristics by City

Variable	Total (N = 305)	Cincinnati (n = 152)	Columbus (n = 113)	Toledo (n = 40)	Probability Level
Race (% black)	48.5	61.2	32.7	45.0	.001
Sex (% female)	70.8	73.0	66.4	75.0	NS
Age (years)	50.6	51.6	48.5	52.9	NS
Education (years)	11.6	11.2	12.1	11.7	.018
Low Income (% < $10,000)	30.6	32.4	24.1	42.1	.093
Currently Married (%)	51.5	54.6	48.7	47.5	NS
Employed (%)	51.8	50.0	55.8	47.5	NS
Contact with Pros (% T1 ever)	68.9	63.8	72.6	77.5	NS
Contact with Pros (% T2, T3)	42.3	42.8	38.9	50.0	NS
NAMI Member (% past and/or present)	9.18	6.58	10.62	15.00	NS

The sample differs from many prior studies of family burden in that when available, multiple family members were interviewed, and the sampling frame was not limited to primary or active caregivers. The distribution of parents was 37 percent; siblings, 25 percent; adult children, 7 percent; and spouses, 3 percent. A variety of secondary kin relations was also represented (19 percent), including small numbers of aunts and uncles, grandparents, nieces and nephews, cousins, in-laws, and the step- and half-relations of blended families. Approximately 10 percent of the respondents were actually "family-like" non-kin. At the first interview with family members, 17.1 percent of family members reported that the client was a member of their household. A further strength of the sample is the ethnic diversity of the family members. Approximately half of the respondents were black and the other half were white.

Table 2.2 reports the descriptive statistics for the family members. Slightly more than two out of three of the family respondents were female. Nearly a third reported household income as less than $10,000 in households that averaged almost three persons, an indication of extreme poverty. Respondents averaged less than 12 years of education, and just over 50 years of age, and about half were currently employed. Approximately half of the respondents were currently married.

Contact with professionals is shown separately in Table 2.2 for those who had contact at some point during their relative's illness, and those who had contact with professionals during the course of the study. As shown, nearly 69 percent reported contact at some point, whereas 42 percent reported contact at T2 and/or T3. Some families had more than one member in contact with professionals. Other families relied on one member to serve as a liaison with the professional system of care, and some families had no member with recent contact with professionals.

Relatively few (9%) of the family respondents were formerly or currently members of a support group for families, such as the National Alliance for the Mentally Ill (NAMI). Further analysis indicated that the percentage of NAMI members (past and present) goes up slightly if limited to mothers (17.4%), and still further if limited to white mothers (26.5%). There was also a significant race difference in NAMI membership; 13 percent of the white respondents were NAMI members compared with only 5 percent of the black respondents.

Multiple respondents were interviewed for a majority of clients at all three points in time. Clients averaged 2.0 respondents at T1, 1.7 respondents at T2, and 1.5 respondents at T3. Compared with family members who dropped out, the 305 family respondents who completed all three interviews were more likely to be female and to be helping the client with activities of daily living. The proportion of clients having more than one family member interviewed declined over the three waves from 61 percent to 51 percent, reflecting a tendency for less involved relatives to drop out of the study. The participation of family respondents also was related to client symptomatology. The higher the level of symptomatology, indicated by a short version of the Symptom Checklist-90 to which the clients responded, the more likely the family respondent was to complete the study.

A NOTE ON SITE AND CLIENT OUTCOMES

There were some significant site differences. Table 2.1 reveals that the lowest proportions of black clients as well as clients diagnosed with schizophrenia are found in Columbus. Clients entering the treatment system in Toledo reported significantly less continuity of care compared with the other two cities. Table 2.2 also compares family member characteristics across the three cities. Cincinnati is distinctive in having a significantly larger percentage of black respondents, as well as those with the lowest education. There tends to be more extreme poverty in the Toledo sample, as indicated by the higher proportion reporting household income under $10,000 (p<.10). Thus, the three sites from which the sample was drawn, although similar in many respects, do differ significantly on race, diagnosis, and the educational attainment of family members.

We should also note that despite much evidence of system change, the client study reported no improvement overall for clients in their quality of life over the course of the demonstration between 1989 and 1991 (Goldman, Morrissey, and Ridgely 1994). Thus, expectations of lower family burden need to be tempered by the lack of positive change at the client level. Still much can be learned from these family members, as the following chapters will show.

Despite its limitations, the sample represents family members who are not often represented in family research. Included are family members whether or not they are caregivers, persons with various ties to the person with mental illness, males and females, blacks and whites, parents and nonparents. In addition, the sample is not limited to members of organized family groups, who, although articulate and involved, are probably not representative of most family members of persons with serious mental illness. All of the clients were also receiving public mental health services, and one-third of the family members had household incomes of less than $10,000 per year. Clearly, the clients were not the only persons under study who were experiencing extreme poverty.

Chapter 3

What Basic Needs Did Family Members Provide?

As we noted in Chapter 1, "Mental Illness and the Family," the post-modern American family has many reasons to relinquish responsibility for caring for the sick to professionals. Particular changes in family structure, notably women's increased participation in the workforce, the rise of single-parent households, and the increasing rate of divorce are at odds with the demands of caring for persons with serious chronic illnesses. The problems of family caregiving are exacerbated in the case of serious mental illness due to the off-timedness of providing long-term care to dependent adults.

Psychiatric patients and their families have learned over the past 40 years that the primary locus of care is the community, and not the hospital. Thus, a major dilemma for family members is how to come to terms with the potential need to provide routine care for adult members who will perhaps never achieve the independent statuses associated with adulthood. What did family members perceive to be the basic needs of consumers? What help did family members of public sector clients provide for their basic needs? Which family members were most likely to come forward? How much did they mind doing these things? As the discussion in this chapter will show, family members assisted the consumer in a variety of ways and expressed a surprisingly limited range of subjective reactions to providing such care.

It is important to begin with the topic of need. Consumers vary in their levels and kinds of need. Diagnosis, symptoms, general level of functioning, compliance with medication treatment, and other factors may be associated with differential needs for care by family members. The family member's perceptions of need may not be the same as the consumer's perceptions or the clinician's. Typically, however, family members will base the support they provide on their own perceptions of need. These may be predicated on something as simple as the consumer asking for help or on something more complicated such as the family member inferring a need even though the consumer has not asked for help.

One of the few studies to examine in detail the everyday life of clients in the community is *Making It Crazy: An Ethnography of Psychiatric Clients in an American Community* by Sue Estroff (1981). This detailed study of 43 clients participating in the Program of Assertive Community Treatment (PACT) in Madison, Wisconsin, will be cited often in the results presented below. We believe that this work provides much insight into consumer life in the community.

Use of the term *family member* to refer to all kin other than the consumer disguises the fact that various family roles have different obligations and rights. Our study employs a broad definition of family, to include secondary kin relations as well as some persons who, while neither related by blood or law, are "like family" according to the clients who nominated them. Even we as researchers were surprised by the large number of types of kin that persons with mental illness can count on for assistance in community living. Clients identified 25 different relationships, including the primary ones of mothers and fathers, husbands and wives, adult sons and daughters, brothers and sisters, and secondary ones such as step-relationships, aunts, uncles, in-laws, and ex-spouses.

These relationships may be viewed as following a hierarchy of obligation. Currently married spouses are most obligated both by custom and law. Parents, although obligated to support their minor children, have a more ambiguous obligation to their adult children. The obligations of adult children, siblings, and more distant kin such as in-laws, cousins, aunts, and uncles, are even more unclear with respect to a relative with mental illness (Farber 1973).

Traditionally, the concept of "family burden" has come to stand for the load that family members carry as they attempt to meet the needs of their relatives with mental illness in the community. This chapter will describe and analyze the distribution of one dimension of family burden—namely, what family members do to provide basic needs for consumers residing in the community. We look at who in the hierarchy of family roles was most burdened and how burden was related to living arrangements. Prior research indicates that the most burden occurs when consumer and family member live together. Although we had less co-residence than was expected in the original research design, it remains a major variable expected to be associated with higher levels of burden.

We hasten to point out that it is not the consumer who is burdensome but rather the caregiving associated with serious and persistent mental illness. The focus in the current chapter is on providing basic needs. The eight areas discussed below do not exhaust all the kinds of care that persons with mental illness may require from family members and others such as providers of mental health services, but the list does represent the most commonly encountered needs.

MEASUREMENT OF FAMILY BURDEN

We begin by describing the needs that may require some assistance with the activities of daily living. Much of the "burden" experienced by relatives of persons with mental illness arises from daily caregiving (Creer, Sturt, and Wykes 1982). Even when florid symptoms of psychopathology are controlled by medication, persons with severe mental illness often experience residual impairments that prevent them from functioning without assistance in everyday life. Many may need help or reminding with such tasks as getting dressed, taking medication, doing laundry, preparing meals, shopping, getting places, managing money, and making use of their time. Consumers living in unsupervised settings or at home frequently rely on a family member to provide such assistance. We conceptualize this dimension as Care.

Our examination of basic needs is grounded in family member responses at the *baseline personal interviews* (October 1989 to March 1990) where the format permitted open-ended questions and encouraged detailed responses. We take both objective and subjective approaches to measuring the burden associated with caregiving in the activities of daily living during the 30 days prior to the interview, examining both what family members did in response to needs they perceived and how they felt about the help they gave. This is only one approach to the measurement of subjective burden, and Chapter 6 will examine other emotional costs experienced by family members.

We presented the family members with the broad list of areas related to Care that are described above. Each area was introduced by two questions that asked for the family member's perception of consumer need. The first question asked if the consumer had *asked* for help in a particular area, and the second asked the family member to state whether the consumer had *needed* help in the area. Family members who responded "no" to both questions were skipped out of that sequence and then coded as having zero burden in that area.

Family members who perceived a need were then asked how often the need had occurred (every day, three to six times a week, once or twice a week, or less than once a week). If need was present, we followed by asking who provided the help. We decided to use four categories that best represented patterns of caregiving: (1) the family member helped by him- or herself alone; (2) someone else helped; (3) the family member helped along with someone else; or (4) no one helped. Family members named a variety of other persons who helped, including case managers, staff at group homes, nurses, and police.

If the family members being interviewed had helped, we asked them how much they minded providing such help (a lot, some, very little, or not at all). For those who minded very little or not at all, we asked, "Why is that? Are you used to it, or what?" Responses other than "used to it" were systematically recorded and are drawn upon in the following analysis.

The major goal of this chapter is to present the family experiences that can often get lost beneath numbers. As we have reported elsewhere and will do again at the end of this chapter, we found low levels of overall burden when looking at the total sample. But to use only summary measures and to include family members who report little need or caregiving within a limited time frame may not adequately represent the family experiences of the most involved relatives. Those family members who reported needs and who provided help to the consumer with various activities of daily living may be considered special populations, and in this section we provide an item-by-item discussion, augmented with qualitative data describing family experiences. Combining quantitative and qualitative methodologies is sometimes the most effective way to present the situations of special populations (Schulz and Biegel 1993).

RESULTS

As we described in Chapter 2, the research presented in this volume is limited to the 305 family members who completed all three interviews. The results are reported below, item by item, for the Care dimension only for those family members who perceived a need and uses only the *baseline* interview data. We first report on those family members who perceived needs and then turn to the more typical analyses, which use summary scales and the total sample.

We anticipate our examination of the individual items by summarizing the rank orderings of the eight areas that make up the dimension of Care. The most *perceived need* of the client-relative was in the area of managing money, followed in descending order by assisting with transportation, making use of time, and helping with medication, then by laundry and household chores, shopping, and personal hygiene. Cooking or preparing meals was last. Family members reported helping the most (either alone or with others) with transportation, followed in descending order by managing money, making use of time, helping with medication, household chores, shopping, personal hygiene, and last, preparing meals or cooking. Family members minded the most about helping with personal hygiene, followed in descending order by making use of time, managing money, helping with household chores, giving rides or helping with public transportation, helping with medication, cooking or preparing meals, and shopping. Table 3.1 reports the items ranked in terms of perceived need as well as by who helped.

We now turn to the individual areas and begin with helping to manage money, which is the area in which family members perceived the most need. We present the number (rather than percent) of family members because of small amounts of missing data in some areas and also because the base changes from area to area, depending on the numbers of family members who perceived a need.

Managing Money

Family members reported the most need in the area of helping the client to manage his or her money. Of the 305 family members, 133

Table 3.1
Caregiving by Individual Items Ranked by Need

Activity	Need for Help	FM* Only Helped	Other Only Helped	FM & Other Helped	No One Helped
Money	133**	41	65	10	17
Transportation	130	28	57	42	1
Time	76	18	22	31	3
Medication	76	19	31	23	3
Housework	72	25	30	16	0
Shopping	72	26	33	13	0
Grooming	53	16	17	20	0
Meals	51	16	25	10	0

Notes: *FM = Family Member; **numbers are frequencies because they do not in all cases add up to the total need for help due to small amounts of missing data.

(44%) stated either that the consumer asked for help with managing money; the family member perceived that the consumer needed help managing money or needed to have it managed for him or her; or replied "yes" to both questions. Of the 133 family members who perceived a need, 53 reported it was needed either every day or three to six times a week.

It is not surprising that managing money is frequently seen as an area where persons with mental illness may need help. Consumers may receive money from various sources, including Supplemental Security Income (SSI), Social Security Disability Insurance (SSDI), veteran's benefits, welfare, and other income maintenance programs (Estroff 1981). Consumers also may participate in paid employment. However, many may be unwilling or unable to manage their money in a way that ensures their basic survival by seeing that such things as rent and utilities get paid. Estroff reported that 16 of the 27 clients receiving SSI had a financial guardian or payee other than themselves (1981). Mental illness can also produce a vulnerability to being exploited financially by confidence schemes, theft, and sometimes poor judgment about other persons and their motives. Behaviors in the manic phase of bipolar disorder may include irrational spending sprees. Indeed, at times relatives with mental illness may "spend money like the 'proverbial drunken sailor' " (National Depressive and

Manic-Depressive Association 1993). Many family members discern a need to help out in this area either formally as a guardian or payee or informally on an ad hoc basis as the need arises. When asked who provided such assistance, 17 family members said no one helped. This represents the consumer's unmet need in the area of managing money as perceived by a family member. This is the largest frequency of all Care areas in which family members perceived that the consumer's needs were not being met by *someone* (including others than themselves). Fifty-one family members reported helping in this area either alone (41) or with others (10). Another 65 reported that someone else had provided help in this area.

Few family members minded helping in this area. Thirty-five (69%) of the 51 family members who helped said they minded very little or not at all. When asked why they minded so little, three-fourths said they were used to it, suggesting they were resigned to helping with money. We asked those who minded very little or not at all but were *not* used to it to say why. These family members responded with a variety of reasons including love, family responsibility, liking to help, and fear of the consumer's circumstances if no one helped. When the eight areas of assistance are ranked in terms of the average scores of how much family members minded, the area of managing money ranked third with an average of .90 (close to very little).

Transportation

The second-most frequently reported need was in the area of giving rides or helping to use public transportation. The need for transportation arises out of one of the basic realities of deinstitutionalization, which is that life in the community requires mobility, and without transportation, clients are inevitably isolated from people, services, and activities. Indeed, family members perceive this as a major need of consumers (surpassed only slightly by the need for help with managing money). Almost 43 percent (130 persons) of the 305 family members stated that the consumer asked for or needed a ride or needed help to use public transportation. Of the 130 family members who perceived a need in this area, more than three-fourths said the need had occurred once or twice a week or less during the last 30 days.

When asked who provided such assistance, only one family member reported that no one helped (unmet need). Fifty-seven family members reported that the help was provided by someone other than themselves (including other family members or friends, etc.). Seventy family members who perceived a need gave help with transportation, either alone (28) or in conjunction with others (42).

Very few family members complained when asked how much they minded helping clients with their transportation needs. The vast majority reported minding very little or not at all. When asked why they minded very little or not at all, family members responded with statements such as they "just didn't mind" or "because I love her." Many circumstances in the lives of clients and their family lead family members to help out in this way. For example, a client's car has broken down, or the client may not have a car at all. One family member stated, "I feel sorry for her because she doesn't have a car." When the eight areas of assistance are ranked in terms of the average scores of how much family members minded, the area of helping with transportation ranked fifth with an average score of .75 (close to very little).

Making Use of Time

The next most prevalent areas of need were helping the consumer make use of his or her time (about 25 percent of family members reported a need) and helping with medication (also about 25 percent and discussed below). Seventy-six family members reported that the consumer needed to be helped, reminded, or urged to make use of his or her time, such as going to work, school, aftercare, or visiting with friends.

According to Agnes Hatfield, a founding member of NAMI, the biggest concern of family members has not changed in almost 20 years. They are still most concerned about the seeming lack of motivation that can become a way of life for some consumers (Hatfield 1994). The clients in the PACT study counted on family members, staff, and other consumers to help fill their days (Estroff 1981). As Estroff noted, for many consumers, there was no concept of "leisure" time, and helping to fill large blocks of unstructured time was a major concern of the staff.

Seventy-six of the 305 family members perceived a need in this area. Just over half perceived the need to be every day or three to six times a week. Three family members perceived this need as unmet by anyone. Twenty-two family members reported that someone other than themselves provided this help. Forty-nine family members reported that they gave help in this area alone (18) or with others (31).

Of the 49 family members who helped in this area, the vast majority responded that they minded very little or not at all. Of these, 70 percent reported they didn't mind helping because they were used to it. Some family members remarked that they did not mind helping in this area because they saw a life constructed around doing nothing as a real loss of potential, and they envisioned that the consumer was capable of doing much more. Others enjoyed the consumers' company and appreciated being able to help.

When the eight areas of assistance are ranked in terms of resentment toward helping, the area of leisure time ranked second, with an average of 1.04 (between very little and some). Helping with leisure time was second only to personal hygiene in terms of how much family members minded.

Medication

As already noted, perceived need for help with medication was equal to the need for help in managing time. However, unlike "making use of time," where there is a potential need for all consumers, not all of the consumers were supposed to be taking medication, although a majority were. Eighty-three percent or 253 family members reported that their relative with mental illness needed to take medicine for his or her problems. Of this group, 76 of the family members said the consumer either asked for help or needed to be helped, or reminded, to take his or her medicine. One-third reported the help was needed every day.

For a variety of reasons, persons with mental illness may not comply with medication regimens. They may forget. Or they may refuse to take medications because of unwanted side effects. A number of family members mentioned as a barrier to medication compliance the consumers' belief that taking prescribed medicine made them fat. Obviously this is a delicate area of negotiation between consumers and family members in which more is involved than simply asking for help. This is also one area in which deciding not to help, or being unable to help, may result in more burden than if one actually did help. Mental health crises are often triggered when a consumer ceases to take his or her medication, and the side effects of abrupt termination may include a ferocious relapse (Baldessarini 1994). When relatives with severe and persistent mental illness refuse or forget to take their psychiatric medications, it is often difficult for family members to continue to care for them in the community (Pasamanick, Scarpitti, and Dinitz 1967).

Three family members perceived that no one helped the consumer although they thought the consumer needed help in this area. Thirty-one family members reported that someone other than themselves helped. Forty-two family members provided help with or reminding about taking medication either alone (19) or with others (23).

Of the 42 who provided help with medication, the vast majority minded very little or not at all. However, six family members minded a lot, and these family members may have expended much effort in negotiating compliance. Of the 33 persons who had minimal complaints in this area, 17 replied they were used to it when asked why they minded so little. Other reasons for not minding included the acceptance of a personal role in the treatment process and a belief that assisting in this area was truly helping the consumer stay well. For some, the task was seen as a duty associated with a family role, as indicated by comments such as "I'm his *father*" or "she's my *mother*." Several family members expressed a fear of decompensation if the medication routine was not followed. When the eight areas of assistance are ranked in terms of the average scores of how much family members minded, the area of helping with medication ranked sixth, with an average of .69 (once again close to very little).

Housework and Laundry

Tied for next place in terms of frequency of need were help with housework or laundry (discussed first) and help with shopping for groceries, clothes, and other things (discussed below). Long-term stays in psychiatric facilities to some extent eliminated the need for family members to help in these areas. With the rise of independent community living, consumers may need family members to remind them to do their housework or laundry, help them with their housework or laundry, or actually do housework or laundry for them. We expected that how family members perceived the need for help with housework and laundry would be related to gender roles, with female relatives both perceiving greater need than male relatives, and giving more help in this area.

Seventy-two family members perceived that consumers needed help in this area. Forty-seven of those who perceived a need stated that it was only once or twice a week or even less. We were somewhat surprised by the low level of need in this area, but doing housework and laundry still tends to be thought of as women's work. Males typically may receive this help from female relatives without having to ask for it. In addition, a mother or a wife may not even perceive a need for this help for her son or husband and just do it automatically as part of her gender role.

No consumer was perceived as having an unmet need in this area. Of the 20 family members who provided this help alone, 80 percent were females. Eighty percent of the 16 family members who provided this help with others were also females. Thirty family members reported that others only helped in this area. Forty-one family members helped in this area either alone (25) or with others (16).

Three-fourths of the 41 family members who were providing help with housework and laundry minded not at all or very little. Of the 30 family members who minded very little or not at all, 22 said they were used to it. Other reasons for not minding were linked to the connection between laundry and cleanliness and the definition of help in this area as part of a family role. One mother explained, "It's a natural thing to bring up." When the eight areas of assistance are ranked in terms of the average scores of how much family members minded, the area of housework and laundry ranked fourth, with an average of .85 (close to very little).

Shopping

The consumer's need for help with shopping for groceries, clothes, and other things was, as noted above, tied with helping with housework and laundry in terms of frequency. Shopping was not a characteristic activity of persons with mental illness during the era of long-term hospitalization. Shopping implies getting to a market and/or store, dealing with salespeople, choosing from an array of merchandise, and staying within a budget. Living in the community requires the consumer of mental health services to also be a consumer of a variety of goods and services.

Seventy-two family members reported that the consumer asked for or needed help with shopping. About 54 percent said the need was less than once a week, and fully 90 percent perceived the need to occur less than once a week or only once or twice a week. Thirty-nine family members helped in this area either alone (26) or with others (13). Thirty-three family members reported a need but that someone other than themselves helped. There was no unmet perceived need in this area.

Only three people minded a lot, two minded some, seven minded very little, and the vast majority minded not at all. When asked why they minded very little or not at all, most replied that they were used to it, implying that many family members become resigned to helping in this way. Others replied that it fits in with their own routines, or that they just like to help out. Three adult children cited their family roles, and one said it is "a good thing for a son to do." When the eight areas of assistance are ranked in terms of how much family members minded, the area of shopping ranked eighth, with an average of .52 (close to very little). This is the area that family members minded the least, perhaps because it did not interfere with their own activities or because they were resigned to helping in this area.

We should note that helping with shopping and helping with transportation are related and that it is difficult to separate the two activities. Indeed, some family members cited shopping as a reason for giving a ride, and some helped with shopping because the consumer's car had broken down or because the consumer had no one else to take them. Shopping may also be linked to a desire to assist consumers with managing their monies, as well as a desire to help them choose more healthful foods.

Grooming, Bathing, and Dressing

Estroff observed that "clients often dressed in soiled, ill-fitting, and ragged clothes.... The usually disheveled and soiled nature of dress, along with a customary lack of attention to style and matching of colors and prints, gave the clients a subtly distinctive appearance.... The staff was concerned with teaching clients acceptable grooming habits, and at times required that a client return home to bathe or to change clothing before going to work or to a job interview" (Estroff 1981, p. 66). It would appear that ignoring culturally expected personal habits may be an expression or at least a corollary of serious mental illness. As such we would expect a substantial need.

But to the contrary, we find that only 53 out of 305 family members reported that the client asked for or needed to be helped or reminded with things such as grooming, bathing, or dressing. When help was needed, it tended either to be needed every day (almost a third of the family members reported a daily need) or only occasionally (almost two-thirds reported once or twice a week or less).

A total of 36 family members helped in this area alone (16) or with others (20), and 17 reported that someone else was involved. Surprisingly, family members perceived no unmet need connected to grooming, bathing, or dressing.

When those 36 family members who helped were asked how much they minded helping, 16 said not at all and another seven said very little. The other 13 reported minding some or a lot. When the 23 were asked why they minded little or not at all, 15 said they were used to it, implying a long term accommodation. The remainder gave other reasons, including duty and love. Another said she liked doing this for her family member, and one said she did it because the consumer likes being clean. When the eight areas of assistance are ranked in terms of the average scores of how much family members minded, the area of grooming, bathing, and dressing ranked first, with an average of 1.11 (between very little and some). This is the area family members minded the most.

As will be discussed in Chapter 4, we believe that some consumers refuse help with their grooming and bathing. These refusals have implications for family members. This is an area where not being allowed to provide assistance may be more burdensome than actually helping. When help is refused, the personal hygiene and inappropriate dress of consumers are important sources of embarrassment for family members. If the consumer accepts help reluctantly, it may be with some resentment and become a source of friction within the family.

Cooking and Meal Preparation

Family members perceived the least need in the area of cooking or preparing meals. Estroff reported that few of the clients in the PACT program in Wisconsin cooked their own meals even though they had access to cooking facilities (1981). Coffee shops, lunch counters, fast-food restaurants, and soup kitchens served the function of preparing or cooking meals. Evidently many consumers are seen by their family members as capable of meeting this basic need on their own. Only 51 family members perceived a need in this area. However, more than half perceived the need as a daily one. No one perceived this as an unmet need.

When asked who did provide help in this area, 26 said they helped alone or with others, and another 25 said someone else did (including staff members at group homes and supervised housing). Only four people out of the 26 minded some or a lot. Of the 22 family members who minded only a little or not at all, 16 said they were used to it. The other six family members who were asked why they minded so little replied with statements such as: "I like to eat. If I eat, you eat"; "I have to cook for myself anyway"; "She couldn't do it herself. It's something I need to do"; "He's my kid—I like to help him"; and "Because I wanted to."

When the eight areas of assistance are ranked in terms of how much family members minded, the area of cooking and preparing meals ranked seventh, with an average score of .53 (again close to very little). Cooking, which ranked seventh, and shopping, which ranked eighth, are the two areas family members minded helping with the least.

THE LARGER PICTURE

Thus far our focus has been on individual items and restricted to those family members who had perceived a need or given care within each area in the past 30 days. In the current section, we expand the scope of the analysis by using the index of total need and scales of objective and subjective Care that encompass all eight areas. We include all 305 sample members irrespective of whether they gave care in the previous 30 days. Summary scales such as the ones reported in this section are the more typical way in which research results are reported.

Distribution of Total Need

We have seen that the need for Care varies from area to area. The most need was reported in the area of managing money and the least with personal hygiene. About 30 percent of family members perceived that their relative with mental illness had no need for assistance with any of the activities of daily living. Fully 50 percent of family members perceived either no need at all or only one need. Of course, even if only one need was reported, it may represent an area of extreme importance to both the family member and the RMI. Approximately 18 percent perceived that the consumer needed help in four or more areas.

Several interpretations may be used to explain the low levels of perceived need that the family members reported. First, the need was restricted to the previous 30 days. Family members indeed often complain about these limited time frames, saying things such as, "He's doing fine now, but you should have asked me six months ago." Second, not perceiving a need may serve as a justification for not providing any assistance. In addition, the areas of Care that we have described may be more apparent when family members live with consumers and interact on a daily basis. Alternatively, the apparent lack of perceived need may suggest the effectiveness of the public system of care.

Distribution of Total Care

A frequency distribution of objective care indicates that 53 percent gave no Care in any of the eight areas, 19 percent gave care in one area, 10 percent gave Care in two areas, and the remaining 19 percent gave Care in three or more areas. Thus, the general picture is one of a relatively low level of burden on any individual family member when measured as assistance with the activities of daily living. We also wish to point out that in few cases were consumers reliant on just one primary caregiver. Helping is an activity that is shared, and in no case did the help provided by a lone family member exceed the help provided to the consumer by others or by the family member in conjunction with other(s).

The distribution of subjective Care was even more skewed. Three-fourths of the 305 family members were not subjectively burdened by providing assistance in these areas. There are at least two reasons for this: One, many family members minded "not at all" when they did provide help. Two, if family members perceived no need, they did not need to help and could not "mind" something they did not provide. Average scores for objective burden were .15 (minimum is 0 and maximum is 1) and for subjective burden .12 (minimum is 0 and maximum is 2.25).

Table 3.2
Objective and Subjective Care by Family Role and Living Arrangements

Variable	n	Objective Care	Subjective Care
Family Role		(mean)	(mean)
Parent	113	.21	.18
Spouse	8	.16	.06
Siblings	77	.12	.11
Adult Children	20	.10	.01
Other Kin	87	.09	.07
Living Arrangements		(mean)	(mean)
Co-resident	52	.26	.18
Not Co-resident	253	.12	.10

Notes: Family Role and Objective Care: F = 5.24; DF = 4,300; p <.001
   Family Role and Subjective Care: F = 2.58; DF = 4,300; p <.05
   Living Arrangements and Objective Care: F = 19.78; DF = 1,303; p <.001
   Living Arrangements and Subjective Care: F = 3.00; DF = 1,303; p <.10

Distribution of Care by Family Role and Living Arrangements

Next, we present the quantitative results of Care and feelings about Care for the total sample broken down by family role and residence. Examination of Table 3.2 reveals that in the 30 days prior to the interviews, parents of sons and daughters with mental illness were significantly more likely to be helping, followed by spouses, siblings, adult children, and other kin. When we turn to subjective Care, the rank ordering differs slightly, with parents also minding significantly more than other relatives, followed by siblings rather than spouses. Adult children minded the least. Evidently, helping with activities of daily living is not evenly distributed among family members, and depends heavily on the duties and obligations associated with the family role. The dislike of helping is also related to family role, with siblings disliking most the help that they provide, presumably because it interferes with the trajectory of their own life course by presenting obligations not typically associated with the role of an *adult* brother or sister.

Although we did not report results for individual items by family role because the limited number of cases was too small to detect statistical significance, we do wish to report one interesting descriptive finding. No adult children helped in the area of managing money. (The reader is reminded that in Chapter 2, we reported that consumers averaged 35.5 years of age and could not be older than 65.) The role reversal involved in children managing their parents' money is evidently less common than in the aging area, where a parent might have a dementia.

Table 3.2 also shows the distribution of Care and the dislike of providing such caregiving depending on whether the family member does or does *not* live with the consumer. Co-resident family members helped in more areas than did non-co-resident family members, helping on average in slightly more than two areas, whereas those who lived apart from the consumer helped on average in less than one area. Those who lived with the consumer also tended to mind helping more, although neither group had high levels of complaints on average.

A substantial proportion of relatives who were *not* living with the client were also involved in Care. A total of 42 percent of non-co-residents (compared with 71 percent of co-resident family members) helped with Care. The overall distribution of Care mirrors the typical patterns of kinship obligation, with spouses (when present) and parents most involved, and siblings, adult children, and secondary kin much less involved. However, residence overshadows family role. When we look at Care provided by family role and living arrangements together, there is no significant difference in help provided by parents, adult children, spouses, siblings, and secondary kin who live with the consumer. Living arrangements do not make a significant difference among the family roles with respect to subjective burden.

DISCUSSION

The central dilemmas of this chapter of whether to help and how much Care to provide a relative with mental illness when community tenure is the prevailing social policy are resolved in various ways. It seems clear that the burden of caring for the client who has serious and persistent mental illness is not evenly distributed within families. Although some kin experience major changes in their daily routines, others appear almost unaffected by the mental illness of their relative, at least for the 30 days asked about in the interview, even though the consumer named them as someone involved in their daily lives. Recall that these family members were to be interviewed two more times over the next two years.

As many as 53 percent of the family members reported no Care during this period. It may be that consumers can draw on many more resources (except when in crisis) than has been previously suggested. In fact, the data on need and intensity support this interpretation in virtually all of the areas considered. An alternative explanation for our failure to document high levels of burden is not the diminution of client need, but rather the diminution of family support in situations in which the limits of generosity and tolerance have been reached. We explore this alternative interpretation further in Chapter 7.

When thinking about the 53 percent who said they did not help in any way, we should remember that answering "no" to the beginning questions in each series does not rule out consumer need. And there are also some Care issues that may be important precisely because family members cannot help, such as personal hygiene. Some family members may feel most burdened when the consumer does not ask for or take help. In addition, some family members may be fearful of finding themselves labeled as overinvolved by mental health professionals, that is, as being involved with the consumer to the consumer's detriment. Other family members need to reconcile their desire to support client freedom and independence while assuring that the client's basic needs are being met. This tension puts a more benign face on many circumstances where family members may choose not to intervene, at least for a time.

A related dilemma, particularly for parents, is inherent in trying to compensate for lack of services without compromising the consumer's independence. Even when help is offered, it is sometimes refused, and this right to refuse receives substantial support from other consumers and consumer advocates. For these reasons, "doing nothing" can sometimes represent a significant part of the family experience.

Family burden research typically looks at only primary caregivers, yet "family" implies more than the dyad of caregiver and care recipient. As we have seen, caregivers often report other persons who provide help, and in all areas help is more likely to be provided by others than by the family member acting alone. In addition, some families divide the labor, producing a network of caregivers. Others may take turns in the role. Siblings may distance themselves in early adulthood only to take up a caregiving role as parents age and die. By contrast, the consumer's parents may find themselves assisting not their son or daughter but instead his or her minor children. Clearly, informal caregiving is oftentimes as complex as the formal system and has its own unique characteristics.

The current chapter has focused on a single aspect of burden, that is, assisting the consumer with the activities of daily living. In some respects the main finding was not the "colossal burden" of mental illness on family members but instead the mild to moderate levels in the area of providing basic needs, and the mild to moderate levels of resentment resulting from helping. Of course, anticipating that one would mind a lot may account for decisions to not provide any help. In the next chapter, we continue to analyze the family experience by turning to the dimension that we call the supervision or Control of bothersome or troublesome behaviors.

Chapter 4

What Troublesome Behaviors Did Family Members Try to Control?

A critical dilemma for family members is posed by the troublesome behaviors that are sometimes associated with mental illness. Very often family members feel the need to do something about the client's bothersome behavior, leading them to take on the role of de facto guardians or controllers of the client. The alternative is to leave this role for the formal systems, which may mean hospitalization or incarceration.

As Harriet Lefley, a researcher and a family member, has stated, "Mental illnesses are the most baffling of human disorders because they are manifested behaviorally rather than physiologically" (1987b, 107). At the very least the behaviors may be embarrassing; at the very most they may be frightening or threatening. As a result, family members may face a range of behavioral problems requiring caregiving decisions that go beyond the realm of the everyday routine events described in Chapter 3. Family members have reported that much of their distress is indeed linked to behavior management issues (Lefley 1987b). In response to behaviors that are bizarre or disruptive, relatives of persons with mental illness may use rational arguments, emotional pleas, threats, or appeals to third parties such as social workers or in extreme cases, the police.

Strategies for managing behavioral problems vary greatly, but they all have in common an effort to seek some measure of control in an attempt to impose order. Of course this does not mean that consumers either want or accept family members' efforts to control their behavior. Thus, a related dilemma for family members is how to control behavior without being seen as hostile, critical, or over involved by both consumers and mental health professionals (Greenley 1986).

Some years ago a group of researchers in Great Britain operationalized the variety of behaviors that require behavioral management under the rubric of "socially difficult behavior" (Creer, Sturt, and Wykes 1982). Although their sample was small, based on interviews with 52 relatives, this was one of the first studies to question a range of family members (e.g., spouse, parent, adult child, other relative) about their experience with the types of behaviors that might require supervision or control. Whereas other researchers have focused on specific areas that fall within the category of socially difficult behaviors, such as violence or substance abuse, the early work of Creer et al. stands alone in conceptualizing what these behaviors have in common and what they represent in terms of objective and subjective burden. This dimension of burden is differentiated from the types of needs covered in the prior chapter that Creer and colleagues referred to as support with problems involving self-care.

We approached the burden associated with supervision or control in the same way as we approached the burden of caregiving associated with assistance in daily living. Following the model provided by Creer and colleagues, with modifications suggested by our prior studies in America, we selected embarrassing behavior, attention-seeking behavior, disturbing behavior at night, threatening or violent behavior, talk or threats (or attempts) of suicide, excessive use of alcohol, and the abuse of drugs such as marijuana, cocaine, amphetamines, or heroin. Also following the earlier research, we view this dimension of the burden associated with mental illness as supervision or Control.

Readers are reminded that in our approach to measuring the burden of caregiving, the family member must provide some help or supervision either alone or with others or he or she is recorded as having zero burden. But again, some issues may be most burdensome when no one does anything precisely because no one can! This is particularly true with issues of Control or supervision. An example may help to make this point more clearly. A 72-year-old mother of a son with schizophrenia is unlikely to be able to physically restrain him if he is threatening suicide. Thus, a major part of her burden may be feelings of extreme helplessness, fear, and even guilt.

Creer et al. reported that such areas of concern as suicide were uncommon. However, issues such as suicidal threats or attempts have to happen only once to forever change the family dynamics. In this earlier research, violence was found to be more prevalent, and some family members felt they were living under the threat of violence even when none had occurred (Creer, Sturt, and Wykes 1982).

Our questions are similar to those posed in the previous chapter. What troublesome behaviors requiring supervision or control do family members report? How much do these behaviors bother them? What supervision do family members provide to consumers? How much do they mind doing something about the behaviors? Which family members are most likely to come forward? And finally, what is the relationship between living together and providing supervision or control?

As before, we provide qualitative data to enrich the quantitative approach. We wish to emphasize that we asked only about behavioral problems during the 30 days prior to the interview. As a consequence we may underestimate the prevalence of these issues over a longer time period. As we have noted before, these more serious behaviors need happen only once to have a devastating effect on the family.

RESULTS

Before turning to individual items, we give an overview of how the areas compare in terms of frequency and intensity. The results are reported below for the 305 family members who completed all three interviews, but as in Chapter 3, we use only the Time 1 interview data.

In addition to quantitative measures of Control, we also collected during the baseline interview some qualitative information about the types of problems and situations that family members encounter. As we noted in Chapter 3, combining quantitative and qualitative methodologies is an enriching way to present the situations of special populations (Minkler and Roe 1993). As we will see, issues of control occur rarely, but when they occur they are an important part of the family experience. The subsample of family members who reported a need for the control or supervision of behavioral problems certainly make up a special population, and in this section we provide a limited qualitative analysis of their experiences. In reporting the quantitative results, numbers may sometimes not add up to the totals presented because of small amounts of missing data on specific items.

Table 4.1 indicates that the most frequently reported area of per-

Table 4.1
Supervision of Individual Behaviors Ranked by Need

Behavior	Need for Supervision	FM* Only Helped	Other Only Helped	FM & Other Helped	No One Helped
Attention-Seeking	61**	24	6	15	16
Embarrassing	49	17	6	14	12
Night Disturbance	46	18	8	10	10
Drinking	41	12	10	2	17
Violence	36	4	11	10	9
Drug Abuse	29	6	4	14	5
Suicide	27	11	6	4	5

Notes: *FM = Family Member; **numbers are frequencies rather than percentages because they do not in all cases add up to the total need for supervision due to small amounts of missing data.

ceived *need* for supervision or control of socially difficult behaviors was that of making excessive demands for attention (20.0%); followed by doing something embarrassing in public or before company (16.1%); the client causing a nighttime disturbance (15.1%); having too much to drink (13.4%); the client injuring or threatening to injure someone (11.8%); and using drugs or pills such as marijuana, cocaine, amphetamines, or heroin (9.5%). Talking about, threatening, or actually attempting suicide was the least frequently reported behavior (8.9%).

Forty-five percent of the 305 family members reported that the consumer had had at least one need for supervision or control during the past 30 days. However, less than 30 percent reported doing something about the behavior either alone or with others.

Excessive Demands for Attention

The most frequently reported behavioral problem was excessive demands for attention. When consumers have few outside interests such as work, sports, hobbies, friends, or participation in voluntary associations, there is the potential for demanding behaviors designed to gain the attention of family members who do have other interests.

Sixty-one family members (20%) reported that the consumer was excessively demanding in this way. Twenty-seven family members reported that the consumer had done something every day or three to six times a week to seek attention.

There are striking differences in the types of behaviors reported when client and family member live together compared with when they live apart. However, the underlying dynamics appear to be the result of the consumer's demand for the family member's time and undivided attention. The 17 family members who lived with the consumer reported having their own activities, such as reading, watching television, talking on the telephone, and sleeping, habitually interrupted. Family members who did not live with the consumer overwhelmingly cited telephone calls from the consumer as a means of gaining attention. Calling every day, sometimes six, seven, or eight times a day, calling late at night, or calling and demanding food, cigarettes, or money were mentioned. Sometimes the demands were for visits. In one case, however, numerous calls were made to tell the family member to stay out of the consumer's life.

With the exception of the last example, these behaviors appear to be part of a pattern whereby the consumer is totally dependent on family members for social interaction and the family member is resistant. Interestingly, separate residences do not mean freedom from excessive demands.

Of the 61 family members who reported a behavior problem, 43 said they were bothered "some" or "a lot" by the behavior. When the 18 who reported minding very little or not at all were asked "why is that?," 16 said they were used to it. Of the 39 family members who said they did something either alone or with someone else about the consumer's attention-seeking behavior, 25 said they minded "some" or "a lot" by having to deal with the behavior. (There were two cases of missing data.) When the 12 who reported minding very little or not at all were asked "why is that?," 11 said they were used to it. Apparently resignation builds up over time toward attention-seeking behavior for some family members.

Embarrassing Behaviors

Behaviors that embarrass family members are those that cause them to become self-consciously distressed by drawing public attention to the manifestations of the illness. In this way, embarrassment is related to the stigma of mental illness, which through association generalizes to family members. As Lefley has stated, "The behaviors of persons with psychotic disorders may further isolate the family, diminish its reputation, and jeopardize relationships with friends and neighbors" (1989, 557). On the other hand, Kreisman and Joy (1974) argued that despite the expectations of social scientists, most family members report little shame.

In our study, 49 family members (16.1%) reported that during the past 30 days the client had done something in public or before company that embarrassed them. When asked what he or she did, family members gave a variety of responses. Behaviors that embarrass family members appear to fall into three categories: (1) concerns that are linked to the appearance or the personal hygiene of the consumer; (2) episodes of verbal inappropriateness; and (3) public occurrences that have the potential to personally discredit the family member.

For example, reports include a daughter with mental illness embarrassing her mother by walking in the streets without wearing any clothing; a brother embarrassing his sister by "just laughing and laughing when there isn't anything to laugh at"; or a mother being embarrassed when her daughter lights up a cigarette in church or steals something small and is then threatened with arrest.

Family members are particularly frustrated by the lack of attention to personal appearance. In particular, sloppiness, not shampooing the hair or bathing, and dressing inappropriately for the weather such as wearing heavy clothing in the summer and light clothing when there is snow on the ground are matters of concern for family members. Cursing and swearing in front of minor children or other inappropriate audiences are also distressing. Such things as a daughter "peeing outside in the street," and a son "dropping his pants" are also reported as sources of embarrassment.

Of the 49 family members who reported a behavioral problem, 44 said they were bothered "some" or "a lot" by the behavior. When the five who reported minding very little or not at all were asked "why is that?," four said they were used to it. Of the 31 family members who said they did something either alone or with someone else about the consumer's attention-seeking behavior, 24 said they minded "some" or "a lot" having to deal with the behavior. When the seven who reported minding very little or not at all were asked "why is that?," all of them said they were used to it. Thirteen family members reported that the consumer had done something every day or three to six times a week in public or before company that embarrassed them.

Nighttime Disturbances

As long ago as 1946, Mary Bosworth Treudley stated that "sleep is as essential as food to family well-being and only less apt to be under attack by the mentally ill person" (p. 242). It is one thing to have one's sleep disrupted by an infant or toddler, but quite another thing to have one's sleep disrupted by an adult family member's troublesome behavior.

A number of the examples of nighttime disturbances were related to attention-seeking behavior. For example, when consumers call in the middle of the night, this is interpreted here as nighttime disturbances even though it may also be motivated by attention-seeking. Other issues that may arise out of behavioral manifestations of the illness include making loud noises, hollering outside, playing the TV too loud, banging on the door, playing music loudly, and "clunking" noisily up and down the stairs while family members are trying to sleep. Family members also expressed concern about smoking-related issues, such as carelessness with lighting materials, burning the carpet, or falling asleep with a lighted cigarette. These behaviors create fear in family members who cannot provide surveillance during the night. One family member said, "I am scared that she will get up at night and turn on the stove." Sleep is also disturbed when family members lie awake worrying about irresponsible and potentially dangerous behaviors as well as by the behaviors themselves.

Of the 46 family members who reported disturbing behavior at night, 38 said they were bothered "some" or "a lot" by the behavior. When the eight who reported minding very little or not at all were asked "why is that?," five said they were used to it. Of the 28 family members who said they did something either alone or with someone else about the consumer's disturbing behavior at night, 19 said they minded having to deal with the behavior "some" or "a lot." When the nine who reported minding very little or not at all were asked "why is that?," seven said they were used to it. Sixteen family members reported that the consumer had done something to disturb people's nighttime rest as often as every night or three to six times a week.

Drinking

In part, the consumer's drinking is a problem for both consumer and family members because the consumption of alcohol may interact adversely with psychoactive medications. Drinking to excess by itself can impair both functioning and judgment. Drinking may also make consumers less inclined to continue taking prescribed medications, which itself increases the risk of relapse. Drinking too much is a problem particularly for younger chronic consumers, and represents a risk posed by community living. Too often, therefore, the family feels it is the informal agent of social control, with the only alternative being formal agents such as the police.

We didn't ask family members to elaborate on the circumstances when the consumer drank too much. But we did ask whether the consumer became abusive or assaultive when he or she had too much to drink and whether the drinking led to a public scene. Of the 41 family members who reported that the consumer had had too much to drink during the past 30 days, 20 said the consumer became abusive and assaultive, and 21 said he or she created a public scene. Fourteen said the consumer became both abusive and assaultive and created a public scene, and 14 said the consumer did neither. Seven said there was a public scene but no abuse, and six said there was abuse but no public scene.

Recall that the clients in the current study could not have a primary diagnosis of substance abuse. Without this requirement, drinking problems would loom even larger. Of the 41 family members who reported that the consumer had had too much to drink, 33 said they were bothered "some" or "a lot" by the behavior. When the eight who reported minding very little or not at all were asked "why is that?," two said they were used to it. Of the 14 family members who said they did something either alone or with someone else about the consumer's drinking, 10 said they minded having to deal with the behavior "some" or "a lot." When the four who reported minding very little or not at all were asked "why is that?," all of them said they were used to it. Twelve family members reported that the consumer had too much to drink as often as every night or three to six times a week.

Violence

Incidents of threatened or actual violence to self or others may occur only rarely, but when they do occur they are of great concern to relatives. Researchers have recently turned their attention to the relationship between mental illness and violence. There does appear to be some association, but contextual variables are important (Hiday 1995).

One study of hospitalized psychiatric patients examined family relationships and sought to find out who in the family is most often the target of violence (Straznickas, McNiel, and Binder 1993). These researchers found that parents were "overrepresented among the victims of violent patients." Other risk factors were the age of the consumer of mental health services (younger patients exhibited more violence), the diagnosis (persons diagnosed with schizophrenia tended to be more violent), and residence (living together was associated with more risk of victimization). The patterns identified in these data suggested that the caregiving role is the most salient factor affecting who in the family is likely to be a victim if the consumer becomes assaultive. In addition, attempting to do something, even if only trying to set limits, was found to precede 17 of the 27 identified assaults.

Another study similarly reported that primary caregivers, particularly mothers who live with an adult offspring with schizophrenia, are at greater risk in part because they are more available as potential targets (Estroff et al. 1994). According to these authors, the most significant finding was "the association between mother-adult child co-residence and violence. This association suggests that the parental activity of the mother, along with her degree of proximity to her seriously mentally ill son or daughter, involvement in the consumer's daily life, and vulnerability, creates the opportunity for violence" (p. 678). Interestingly, fathers were rarely if ever chosen as the victim even when co-resident.

Examples of violent acts reported for the 30 days prior to interview in our study included hitting, slapping, pushing, kicking, striking, choking, and fighting. Sometimes the family member reported the threat of violence, which understandably tended to be very distressing. Violence toward property was also felt as threatening.

Of the 36 family members in the study, including 14 mothers who reported that the consumer struck or injured someone or threatened to strike or injure someone, 27 said they were bothered "some" or "a

lot" by the behavior. When the 9 who reported minding very little
or not at all were asked "why is that?," 7 said they were used to it.
Of the 14 family members who said they did something either alone
or with someone else about the threatening or violent behavior, 10
said they minded having to deal with the behavior "some" or "a lot."
When the four who reported minding very little or not at all were
asked "why is that?," all said they were used to it. Four family members reported that the consumer had acted violently or made threats
as often as every day or three to six times a week during the prior 30
days.

Drug Abuse

Substance abuse involving such drugs as crack cocaine and heroin
has devastating effects on family relationships. Abuse of drugs may
alter the user's personality, lead him or her to withdraw from the
family, eliminate the sense of personal responsibility, result in a financial drain, and lead to problems with the police. For these reasons,
family members are understandably very concerned when they sus-
pect drug abuse.

Drug use tends to be related to where the consumer of mental
health services lives. Consumers often are forced to live in urban
neighborhoods that are unsafe in part because they provide easy access to drugs and to drug users. Moreover, the philosophy behind
some supported housing programs that respect the independence of
the consumer, ironically, makes it more difficult to detect drug abuse,
and thus harder to control (Cohen and Sommers 1990). Sometimes
the problem is not detected until a social worker comes to call and
observes that the furniture has disappeared, presumably to support
the drug habit.

A total of 29 family members in the current study stated that they
believed the consumer had used drugs or pills such as marijuana,
cocaine, amphetamines, or heroin during the past 30 days. When
family respondents were asked to explain the basis of their suspicions,
they made the following types of observations: (1) the appearance of
the person, such as the consumer's actions, eyes, marks in veins, etc.;
(2) past patterns of drug use—for example, the person did it in the
past, and their current company includes known drug users; (3) physical evidence, such as finding a vial in the consumer's clothing, hy-
podermic syringes used by a diabetic family member disappear; or (4)

inferring a drug habit based on not knowing where the consumer's money was going.

Of the 29 family members who reported a problem with drug abuse, 25 said they were bothered "some" or "a lot" by the behavior. When the four who reported minding very little or not at all were asked "why is that?," only one replied "used to it." Of the 20 family members who said they did something either alone or with someone else about the consumer's drug abuse, 17 said they minded having to deal with the behavior "some" or "a lot." When the three who reported minding very little or not at all were asked "why is that?," only one responded "used to it." Eight family members reported that the consumer had used drugs as often as every day or three to six times a week.

Suicide

One of the most profound behavioral manifestations that family members must deal with are suicidal threats and attempts associated with depression, mania, and psychosis. They are also linked to the lack of motivation and disappointment that so often accompany the consumer's recognition that his or her illness is long-term. The less consumers are able to work, to socialize, and to marry and have children, the less likely they are to feel that life is worth living.

Although the least frequent area was trying to prevent or stop the client from talking about, threatening, or actually attempting suicide, the behaviors that were reported are serious. Family members reported that suicide threats are linked to feeling unloved and isolated by the illness. Others cited major negative life events such as losing custody of children. Sometimes, drinking too much is viewed as the culprit. One family member described an incident in the past 30 days in which the consumer "had a knife and threatened to cut his wrist, was really drunk that night, and right after that he passed out." It would seem that some suicidal attempts result from psychotic delusions of hearing voices, or from depressive episodes leading to extreme demoralization reflected in refusing to eat or drink.

Of the 27 family members who reported that the consumer talked about, made threats to commit, or actually attempted suicide, 24 said they were bothered "some" or "a lot" by the behavior. Both family members who reported minding "very little" or "not at all" reported that they were used to it. Of the 15 family members who said they did something either alone or with someone else about the behavior, 11 said they minded having to deal with the behavior "some" or "a lot." When the four who reported minding very little or not at all were asked "why is that?," only one responded "used to it." Three family members reported that the consumer had talked about suicide or made threats or attempts as often as every day or three to six times a week.

Distribution of Care by Family Role and Living Arrangements

Next we present quantitative results broken down by type of relationship and living arrangements. The reader is reminded that our sample consisted of 8 spouses, 113 parents, 20 adult children, 77 siblings, and 87 secondary kin relationships (including family-like friends). Fifty-two family members lived with the consumer of mental health services. In reading the following analysis, it is important to control for perceived need. When need for supervision in all seven areas is used to create a total score, perceived need varies significantly by family role. Not surprisingly, parents reported the most perceived need followed by siblings, adult children, and friends. There was no significant association between perceived need and living together.

Examination of Table 4.2 reveals that in the 30 days prior to the interviews, the same pattern of caregiving found with helping with activities of daily living was found to hold true for behavior management. Parents of sons and daughters with mental illness were significantly more likely to be supervising, followed by spouses, siblings, adult children, and lastly, other kin.

We remind the reader that there are two subjective burden measures for supervision and control, unlike the previous chapter, in which there was only one. When we turn to minding the behavior, the rank ordering differs slightly (as was true for subjective burden associated with Care), with parents minding significantly more than other relatives, followed by siblings rather than spouses. However, "secondary relatives" minded the least, unlike Care, where adult children minded the least. Parents minded dealing with the behavior the most, followed by spouses, siblings, adult children, and other relatives.

As was true for Care, providing supervision is not evenly distributed among family members, and depends heavily on the duties and obligations associated with the family role. Attitudes toward the be-

Table 4.2
Supervision Burden by Family Role and Living Arrangements

Variable	n	Supervises	Minds Behavior	Minds Supervising
Family Role		(mean)	(mean)	(mean)
Parent	113	.113	.431	.241
Spouse	8	.089	.268	.179
Siblings	77	.078	.314	.160
Adult Children	20	.050	.221	.079
Other Kin	87	.030	.198	.059
Living Arrangements				
Co-resident	52	.129	.379	.261
Not Co-resident	253	.064	.304	.135

Notes: Family Role and Objective Supervision: $F = 4.21$; $DF = 4,300$; $p < .01$
   Family Role and Minds Behavior: $F = 2.91$; $DF = 4,300$; $p < .05$
   Family Role and Minds Supervision: $F = 3.70$; $DF = 4,300$; $p < .01$
   Living Arrangements and Objective Supervision: $F = 8.47$; $DF = 1,303$; $p < .01$
   Living Arrangements and Minds Behavior: *Not Significant*
   Living Arrangements and Minds Supervision: $F = 5.63$; $DF = 1,303$; $p < .05$

havior are also related to family role, with siblings second only to parents in minding the behavior. It is the family of origin that appears to suffer the most subjective burden related to the behavioral manifestations of mental illness.

Table 4.2 also shows the distribution of supervising behavior and the dislike of both the behavior and of providing supervision, depending on whether the family member does or does not live with the consumer. Co-resident family members were involved almost twice as much as were non-co-resident family members. There was no significant difference in *minding the behaviors* between co-resident and non-co-resident family members, however, those family members who lived with the consumer *minded helping* significantly more than those who were not co-resident.

Thus far we have focused on bivariate results looking at caregiving and family role and caregiving and living arrangements. It is possible that these effects are not independent of each other. To rule out this possibility we used a model to look at the effects of family roles when controlling for living arrangements on both caregiving and subjective distress. The basic pattern is that the family roles of parent and sibling and living with the consumer are all significant predictors, with parent being the most important. Thus, parents (and siblings, although the magnitude of the effect is weaker) do more behavioral management and mind it more both when they share a household with the consumer and when they don't. This basic pattern holds even when controlling for the sex, race, and age of the family member, and the sex of the consumer.

DISCUSSION

Family members resolve the critical dilemma of dealing with the troublesome or bothersome behaviors associated with mental illness in various ways. Perhaps the simplest way is not to perceive any need in these areas. Our measure of need in these areas is based on family members' perceptions. Another way of resolving the dilemma is to acknowledge the need but to deny or minimize that it is bothersome. Some family members rely upon others to help the consumer or enlist others as part of a helping network. Those who do help (alone or with others) may accommodate over time as a coping mechanism and become resigned to certain behaviors that most of us would find intolerable. Resignation is not necessarily negative if it allows family members to resolve the dilemma of controlling behavior without being seen as hostile, critical, or overinvolved (Greenley 1986).

Being a parent or a sibling appears to be related to taking on the role of guardian or controller. Parents routinely exercise behavior management for their own minor children, and siblings (particularly the older ones) often take care of their brothers and sisters. This prior experience may make it easier to take on the caregiving role around behavior management for the adult son or daughter or adult brother or sister. Perhaps this is one reason why parents (and siblings to a lesser extent) may find themselves labeled as overinvolved by mental health professionals. In contrast, spouses and friends are expected to hold equal positions with regard to one another. The role reversal associated with supervising a parent tends to make it less likely that adult children will see a need or try to manage a parent's behavior even if they perceive a problem.

This is not to say that because adopting a caregiving role comes more naturally to parents and siblings, they do not resent both the behaviors and having to do something about them. In addition, because the supervision is based on the family member's perception, it may be neither wanted nor accepted by the consumer, who, after all, is an adult.

Burden research often skips over the behavioral management side of caregiving, focusing instead on activities of daily living and subjective burden. However, not surprisingly, family members were bothered more by supervising behaviors than they were about helping with the activities of daily living, even though these needs are less frequent than more everyday activities.

One final point should be emphasized. In the area of Control, family members report more unmet consumer need than they report in the area of Care (see Chapter 3). There are some things that family members should not be expected to do, and sometimes it appears that no one else is meeting that need, either. Some troublesome behaviors, such as drinking too much, may be uncontrollable either in the informal or formal systems of care.

Chapter 5

How Much Did Family Members Spend?

In this chapter we report how family members coped with the financial dilemma of deciding whether, how much, and for what purpose, to give money to their relatives with mental illness. Did community care require expenditures by family members for mental health services expenses? Or was money given to relatives with mental illness to enhance their personal comfort or even to ensure their basic survival? How did family members respond if their own resources were scarce, and what factors contributed to giving money? The Economic Burden of paying money out of one's own pocket represents an area where generosity is particularly tested.

Chapters 3 and 4 reported what family members did to provide basic needs and supervise the troublesome behaviors that may be associated with mental illness. However, it is important also to take into account how the economic resources of family members are affected. Families, who potentially bear many of the financial costs of keeping their relatives with mental illness in the community, may be impacted positively, negatively, or not at all by an improved service delivery system to their relative with mental illness. In this chapter, we evaluate whether and in what ways family members did or did not reduce financial outlays and thus suffer or benefit economically from changes in the delivery system encouraged by the RWJ initiative.

We present detailed data on the Economic Burden represented by the financial expenditures made by the 305 family members on behalf of their relatives at two points in time; our first measurement asked about the 30 days prior to the first interview in 1989, and the second inquired about the 30 days prior to the last interview in 1992. The time period spans a two-year interval marking the period in which the program was being implemented. We also report who in the family was giving, what expenses they were paying for, and how co-residence was associated with financial support. In addition, we examine other factors affecting Economic Burden, including whether the relative with mental illness is male or female, whether he or she has a history of being homeless, and finally, what family members think have caused their relative's problems.

ECONOMIC BURDEN

As noted in Chapter 1, Economic Burden may take various forms. Earnings may be lost because of the illness of a spouse who is a wage earner. Time spent on caregiving may also carry opportunity costs, for example, by restricting the hours available for paid employment, or for engaging in other activities related to advancing one's career. The mental illness of an adult son may result in his mother not returning to the workforce full time as she had anticipated. There may also be in-kind assistance given by family members such as housing the relative, putting food on his or her table, or shopping for him or her, without money changing hands directly. Most directly, there may be out-of-pocket expenditures paid by family members. Depending on the financial resources of the potential donors, mental illness may lead to a (relative) substantial outlay of money for both health care costs and personal expenditures. It is these direct dollar costs that are the focus of this chapter.

Prior studies suggest that the financial burden is quite considerable. The Economic Burden on primary family members has been documented both when clients and family members live together and when they do not (Franks 1990; Clark and Drake 1994). Clark reported that people with mental illness and substance use disorders clearly received more financial assistance from their families than a comparison group of adults of similar ages in the same neighborhood who did not have a chronic illness (1994). But these samples have been largely drawn from white middle-class parents and have not been diverse with respect to the race, income, and role of family members; have not used the same measurement approach; and have not looked at expenses over time.

WHAT FACTORS CONTRIBUTE TO FAMILY MEMBERS HELPING OUT FINANCIALLY?

We reasoned that the same logic applies to giving the client money as it does to giving care or supervision. We expect that financial contributions to an adult relative vary by kinship roles. As we have noted in previous chapters, primary and secondary kinship roles are associated with different kinds and degrees of responsibilities and obligations. The economic ties between parents and children are perhaps the strongest and are asymmetrical when the child is a minor with employed parents obligated by law to support minor children. The obligation to financially support an adult child with a major mental illness may be felt as a "moral" rather than a legal obligation. The financial ties between married spouses are also among the strongest and upheld in custom and law. All other kinship relationships carry weaker or nonexistent financial obligations. However, even within a given role, such as that of parent, other factors such as co-residence and the attributions family members make about behaviors may affect financial contributions to an adult child with mental illness.

Again, residence is presumed to be an important predictor of financial burden. Co-residence should be associated with greater opportunities for family members both to observe financial needs and to respond to consumer demands.

How dependent and troublesome behaviors are interpreted and the *attributions* that underlie such interpretations may also affect the willingness of family members to give money to relatives with mental illness. Greenley (1986) suggested that how family members conceptualize the patients' difficulties, and their assumptions about the presence of an illness, are related to whether or not they believe the problematic behaviors are under voluntary control. Research by Medvane and Krauss has also suggested that when family members perceive mental illness as similar to physical illness, they tend to have better relationships with their "ill" relative (1989). Accordingly, we hypothesized that family members would be more likely to provide at least some financial support if they attributed their relative's behavioral problems and needs for assistance in daily living to an illness over which the relative had little control and, thus, for which he or she could not be held personally responsible. Conversely, when family members viewed troublesome or dependent behaviors as under the relative's control, we hypothesized that they would be less inclined to give financial support.

Although the unraveling of the kinship bond has long been suspected to play a role in the epidemiology of homelessness, the connection between kinship and homelessness has been little studied (Hatfield, Farrell, and Starr 1984; Lefley, Nuehring, and Bestman 1992). A supportive family network appears to offer some protection against episodes of homelessness for persons with mental illness. A study comparing homeless psychiatric patients with patients who had never been homeless reported that episodes of adult homelessness were related to histories of foster care, due in large part to the foster parent role and responsibility ending when the foster child turns 18 years of age (Susser et al. 1991).

However, as we noted in Chapter 1, relationships between persons with mental illness and their family members may vacillate between periods of closeness and periods of separation (Stoneall 1983). Often this may occur when the family member views the client as not complying with the "rules" on which the family member conditions his or her support or when behavioral problems become intolerable. Episodes of homelessness may result during these temporary estrangements, leaving a residual strain in the relationship and the family member less likely to extend a helping financial hand in the future.

Much family burden research has depended on NAMI samples of family members. Although schizophrenia is diagnosed in equal numbers among men and women, members of NAMI are three times more likely to be the parents of sons rather than daughters (Sommer 1987). Sommer's analysis of data collected from more than 600 parents belonging to the California Alliance for the Mentally Ill indicates that the "most reasonable explanation [for the greater involvement of parents of sons with schizophrenia] is the greater propensity for antisocial behavior on the part of sons, leading to increased parental need for support and outside assistance" (1986–1987, 57). Sons and other male family roles should thus receive more assistance from their family members because of their perceived greater need.

Finally, in some of the analyses reported below, the amount of money given (in dollars) at Time 1 is included as a control variable. Our rationale is that money given reported at the baseline interview represents a propensity to give. Controlling for this amount allows us to see the effect of the other variables on the changes in amounts given at Time 3.

RESEARCH QUESTIONS

In this chapter we will test hypotheses regarding co-residence and kinship role, and explore relationships for the other variables. Our goals are to examine the following questions: (1) how much money is being given and for what types of expenses; (2) are families paying for treatment-related expenses, or is their giving related to everyday expenses (if the mental health system is doing its job, we would not expect either category of expenditures to be large); (3) do the same factors of co-residence and kinship roles that affect other dimensions of family burden also affect financial expenditures; (4) does accepting the medical model of illness make a difference; and finally, (5) do client characteristics (e.g., client need and sex) have an effect.

MEASUREMENT

Direct dollar amounts given to a client have proved difficult to measure because the money may come from different family members, and any given member may be unaware of what someone else has given. In addition, there is the issue of time frame for response. Shorter periods, such as the past month, yield more reliable reports, but may be unrepresentative. Adult family relations with persons with mental illness tend to be accordionlike, coming in and out of closeness, and giving may not be regular (Stoneall 1983).

As with other dimensions of burden, various approaches have been used. The subjective aspect has been least developed. The problem is that what feels like a lot to one person may feel far less burdensome to someone else. Objective approaches range from entire interviews devoted to financial expenditures where the informant provides proxy data for the rest of the family, as in the work of Clark and Drake (1994), to a series of questions addressed to the respondent him- or herself, as in the work of Franks (1990). Although we have not solved all the methodological problems, we do go beyond single caregivers to interview multiple family members (although we report results for individual family members), describe a sample that is diverse with respect to income and race, and measure financial expenditures at two points in time.

The survey questions we used included as expense categories transportation, clothing, pocket money, food, rent, medication, mental health treatment, other medical expenses, cigarettes, personal items, and "other" expenses. Family respondents were asked if during the past 30 days they had personally paid for, or given their relative with mental illness money for each of the above categories; if they responded affirmatively, they were asked to give a dollar amount. The data thus include both a count of the areas in which money was given and total dollar amounts.

Summary economic measures were constructed by adding up the dollar amounts (or the number of areas) over all 11 areas. These data have been further sorted into two categories of expenditures—dollars given for the consumer's personal needs and dollars given for his or her medical and mental health treatment. When respondents said "yes" they gave money, but were unsure of the amounts, we used median substitution to replace the "don't know" codes. We believed this was most conservative and less sensitive to outliers.

To assess the validity of reported amounts, we looked at all values above $50, except for food (food expenditures can run high, and we assumed that $50 or even more is a reasonable amount to give for food over a 30-day period), and cross-checked the amounts with income and the interviewer assessments. We chose not to *impute* a dollar figure for rent when the client lived with the family member, but instead to regard this as an "in-kind" expenditure. We checked the reliability of any report that appeared to be an outlier, checking these against household income and the interviewer's rating of the respondent's truthfulness. We also used median substitution where there was missing data, so long as there were enough cases on which to compute a sample median. When possible, we did the substitution separately under the conditions of co-residence and separate living arrangements.

The items for the attribution module are contained in the Toolkit for Evaluating Family Experience with Severe Mental Illness (Tessler and Gamache 1995b). We asked family members if statements such as, "My relative could have controlled *some* of (his/her) difficult behavior if (he/she) had really wanted" were (1) "definitely not true," (2) "probably not true," (3) "probably true," or (4) "definitely true." Attribution has a mean of 2.33 (between probably not true and probably true) and a Cronbach's alpha of .835.

RESULTS

Before presenting the results of our statistical analyses, we begin with two vignettes to help bring the experience of our family members to life. (Details have been slightly changed to protect the confidentiality of the family members.) These two vignettes illustrate the range and variety of financial expenditures on behalf of relatives with mental illness in a way that gives economic family burden a human face.

Vignettes

An elderly parent has an adult child with a diagnosis of schizophrenia who had been hospitalized for mental illness for less than a month prior to the client study. The adult child has a payee and lives alone in an apartment. The adult child has income from Supplemental Security Income (SSI) and Social Security Disability Insurance (SSDI) but reported no earned income or money from the family. There was no continuous case management for the adult child over the course of the client study. When interviewed in 1989, the parent reported giving the adult child a total of $283 in the past month ($15 for transportation, $30 pocket money, $125 for food, $172 for rent, $40 for cigarettes, $25 for personal items, $22 for a utility bill, and $26 for a telephone bill). The parent stated that both the mother and father make sure that their adult child takes medications and that they share responsibility for managing their child's money. They worry because people take advantage of their child because s/he doesn't know how to manage money. Both parents go every day to check on their adult child.

When we interviewed the same parent in 1992, he reported having given a total of $290 in the past month to his adult child, of which $25 was for pocket money, $60 for food, $175 for rent, and $30 for cigarettes. This parent stated that the other parent (also elderly) gave an unknown amount of money for clothing and personal items. Although we did not interview the other parent, it appears that the consumer's elderly parents are providing both the care and the financial support that enable this consumer to live in the community.

Another family member is the middle-aged parent of a 31-year-old child with a depressive disorder. The divorced child lived alone in an apartment supported by public monies throughout the study. In 1989, the parent, who was then working, made no financial contributions at all to the consumer. However, the parent helped out with transportation by driving the consumer's children to see him on weekends because the consumer did not have a car. In 1992, despite the fact that the parent was no longer working, she reported giving $5 for bus fares in the past 30 days and $2 for pocket money. She has continued to give rides to the consumer, whom she drives to the doctor and to shop for groceries, but the consumer pays for the gasoline. The parent said that once in a while, she also bought a carton of cigarettes for the child, but not within the last 30 days.

Statistical Findings

When we look at the numbers of respondents who gave money in any of the 11 areas in 1989, we find that 43.6 percent made no financial contributions at all on behalf of their relative with mental illness. Among the co-resident family members, the largest numbers gave in the areas of food (77%), cigarettes (42.30%), pocket money (38.50%), and transportation (32.70%). The most frequent areas of giving among non-co-resident family members were the same. However, there were no appreciable differences between the areas, as in general just over one-fifth gave within each of these areas. Average dollar amounts expended over the 30 days prior to interview are also shown for each category of expense, and for both co-resident and non-co-resident family members.

When we look at the numbers of respondents who gave any money in any of the 11 areas in 1992, we find that 66.2 percent made no financial contributions at all. Among the co-resident family members, the largest numbers gave in the areas of food (50%), cigarettes (40%), pocket money (32.50%), and transportation (32.50%). Among the non-co-resident family members, the largest proportions gave pocket money (12.80%), cigarettes (12.10%), transportation (9.40%), and food (7.90%). Once again, average dollar giving for the 30 days prior to interview are shown for each category of expense, and for both co-resident and non-co-resident family members.

Examination of the results in both 1989 and 1992 reveals that regardless of whether they were living together or apart, there was only a modest amount of financial giving. What little giving there was tended to be for personal expenditures—food, pocket money, trans-

Table 5.1
Family Expenditures in 1989

Type of Expense	Co-Resident (n = 52)		Not Co-Resident (n = 253)		Total Dollars
	% Who Gave in Past 30 Days	Amount Given in Past 30 Days	% Who Gave in Past 30 Days	Amount Given in Past 30 Days	30 Day Totals
Transportation	32.70	$10.00	20.20	$3.18	$4.34
Clothing	19.20	$8.27	5.50	$2.57	$3.54
Pocket Money	38.50	$9.33	22.10	$3.64	$4.61
Food	77.00	$68.06	20.00	$3.88	$14.80
Rent	0.00	$0.00	2.80	$4.18	$3.47
Medication	11.50	$7.12	1.00	$0.18	$1.36
Mental Health Treatment	5.80	$1.21	0.00	$0.00	$0.21
Other Medical Expenses	5.80	$2.52	1.20	$0.35	$0.72
Cigarettes	42.30	$11.75	21.30	$1.85	$3.53
Personal Items	19.20	$2.15	7.50	$1.00	$1.19
Other Expenses	1.90	$1.92	6.70	$3.15	$2.94
Total (N = 305)	86.50	$122.31	50.20	$23.97	$40.74

portation, clothing, and cigarettes. Family members spent almost nothing for medication, mental health treatment, and other medical expenses.

Financial outlays were especially low when the relative with mental illness did not live with the family. Families had given more money in the past month to their relative with mental illness if the relative had been living with them ($122 in 1989; $88 in 1992) than if they were living apart ($24 in 1989; $20 in 1992). Even without imputing rental dollars under the condition of co-residence, there is a strong co-residence effect overall (data not shown).

Table 5.3 shows how, as expected, giving was structured by kinship. Although there were only eight spouses, their dollar giving was far and away the highest, followed by expenditures by parents and adult children. Not surprisingly, the least expenditures were reported by siblings and other (more distant) kin. The identical rank order of dollar giving by kinship category was obtained at both points in time.

Table 5.2
Family Expenditures in 1992

| Type of Expense | Co-Resident FMs (n = 40) | | Non-Co-Resident FMs (n = 265) | | Total Dollars |
	% Who Gave in Past 30 Days	Amount Given in Past 30 Days	% Who Gave in Past 30 Days	Amount Given in Past 30 Days	30 Day Totals
Transportation	32.50	$6.50	9.40	$3.75	$4.11
Clothing	25.00	$11.80	5.30	$2.42	$3.65
Pocket Money	32.50	$7.58	12.80	$2.55	$3.21
Food	50.00	$50.25	7.90	$2.02	$8.34
Rent	0.00	$0.00	1.50	$2.70	$2.35
Medication	7.50	$2.00	0.38	$0.04	$0.30
Mental Health Treatment	0.00	$0.00	0.00	0.00	$0.00
Other Medical Expenses	2.50	$1.25	0.38	$0.19	$0.33
Cigarettes	40.00	$7.05	12.10	$2.04	$2.70
Personal Items	10.00	$1.43	4.90	$1.62	$1.59
Other Expenses	0.00	$0.00	3.40	$3.06	$2.66
Total (N = 305)	75.00	$87.85	27.55	$20.37	$29.22

Table 5.3 also gives (in the bottom row) the annualized estimates of giving. The results indicate that there was a statistically significant decline in total monthly dollar amount given between 1989 ($40.74) and 1992 ($29.22), with the decline appearing to be related to the decline in co-residence (df = 304, t = 2.15, p = .03).

Despite the decline in expenditures, the results do show some continuity in the disposition to give money to a relative with mental illness. That is, giving money, as measured in dollars given at one point in time, does significantly predict future giving. Financial outlays are an extension of a family role and relationship with an ill relative and, as such, is more predictable than it is capricious. When giving does occur, it is related to family role, with spouses and parents feeling more obligated to give than other family members.

Related analyses reveal that giving is further structured by how family members interpret their relative's mental illness, with more

Table 5.3
Kinship and Economic Burden

Relationship	n	1989 Giving	1992 Giving
Spouse	8	$190.88	$75.88
Parent	113	$61.06	$55.59
Adult Child	20	$49.35	$31.70
Siblings	77	$25.82	$9.34
Other Kin	87	$11.76	$7.70
Total	305	$40.74	$29.22
Estimated Annual Expenditure		$488.88	$350.64

Notes: Time 1: $F = 13.01$; df = 4,300; p = .0000
Time 3: $F = 8.04$; df = 4,300; p = .0000

money given when the giver views the behaviors associated with mental illness as outside the client's control, and less money given if the relative with mental illness has been homeless. Although homelessness may signify financial need, it may also signify that a process of disengagement between the family and the ill relative has already taken place. Finally, and unexpectedly, male relatives with mental illness received more financial assistance from family members than female relatives.

DISCUSSION

When annualized by multiplying by 12 (months), the yearly amounts of expenditures average $489 in 1989 and $351 in 1992. Annualizing for family members who are living with ill relatives, where expenditures are highest, results in $1,464 in 1989 and $1,054 in 1992. Considering the extreme poverty that characterizes many of the family members (recall that about 30 percent reported household income as less than $10,000), this magnitude of giving is not at all trivial. For many family members, it probably exceeds 10 percent of their total available income.

Many of the findings were expected. Co-residence is a consistent correlate of family burden, as we have seen in prior chapters, and so the higher expenditures under the condition of co-residence provides additional confirmation of its important role in structuring the family experience. Similarly, the effect of family role on expenditures further supports the significance of parenthood compared with most other family ties. The only possible exception is being a spouse.

Likewise, the findings that families gave more money when they construed their relatives' problems as owing to illness rather than lack of effort, and that relatives with a history of homelessness also received less money from kin, were also anticipated. But in both cases, it is difficult to choose between alternative interpretations. Was the person with the disorder seen as an unworthy recipient of family monies because he or she was not trying harder to get better, or was blaming the relative with mental illness by some a way to reduce the dissonance of not contributing, or not contributing more, financially? By the same token, was it the stigma of homelessness that led family members to give less money, or was it low family giving that contributed (along with other factors) to homelessness?

The finding that is most difficult to interpret is that male relatives with mental illness received more money than female relatives. That females tended to receive less money from family members runs counter to the cultural assumption that females are more vulnerable than males, and thus more in need of financial support from kin. We examined various factors to understand why females received less money from relatives, but none satisfactorily explained the difference. The disparity between the sexes was not due to differences in co-residence, attribution (illness versus lack of effort), family role, or homelessness.

The decline in financial expenditures may be good news for the RWJ Foundation's program. None of the other dimensions of burden discussed in Chapters 2 (Care) and 3 (Control) showed a significant decline. Only dollar giving declined between 1989 and 1992. When dollar giving did occur, it was also appropriate, considering the mission of the public mental health system to protect families from the colossal expenses associated with treatment, medication, and specialized housing arrangements. Thus, the pattern of financial giving suggests that the public mental health system may be reaching at least one of its goals, that is, to buffer family members from at least those costs that are directly related to their relative's mental illness.

Chapter 6

What Were the Emotional Costs for Family Members?

In Chapters 3, 4, and 5, we described three objective dimensions of the family burden: providing assistance with the activities of daily living (Care), supervising troublesome behaviors (Control) and helping out financially (Economic Burden). But family members also may need to deal with the distressing negative emotions that may arise from the family experience with mental illness. As we have seen, many family members did extend themselves for their relative with mental illness. However, another dilemma for family members arises when subjective burden conflicts with the role of caregiver.

To illustrate the strong negative feelings that family members sometimes experience, we begin with a brief sample from a much longer list of comments and observations made by and about the relatives who participated in the RWJ family study. The following qualitative material indicates how some family members express their individual psychological costs. An interviewer for the family study described a parent as "caring to the point of tears" and "crushed by the fate of an adult child." Another parent referred to the "frustration and stress," and yet another recounted "all the pain of the past two years," expressing anger and outrage at the mental health system. A sibling reported being angry at all the attention that a brother with mental illness received. A spouse reported that she has only one person, her adult child, with whom she talks and that "she doesn't feel close to anyone." Another relative reported that abusive behaviors make the entire family want to "run and hide."

At times, consumer empowerment and noncompliance may come into conflict with family aspirations for a more symptom-free life for the family member with mental illness. When this occurs, the family burden is not so much what relatives actually do for the consumer; rather, the impact comes from what consumers refuse to let family members do for them. Family members report feeling bothered and frustrated when consumers refuse to comply with professionally pre-scribed regimens. A mother, when asked if she reminded her daughter to take her medicine, replied, "She just won't take it; she doesn't think she needs it" and predicted that her daughter would be back in the hospital in six weeks.

The emotional costs of caring for a person with mental illness can be overwhelming even in the absence of objective caregiving. Recall the embarrassing behaviors described in Chapter 4, such as a relative walking in the street without wearing any clothing, lighting up a cig-arette in church, or stealing. As we have seen, some family members are also embarrassed by the personal appearance of the consumer when they fail to observe rudimentary rules of cleanliness and appro-priate dress. The costs of some behaviors associated with mental ill-ness are incurred precisely because family efforts to help are spurned.

Thus, the psychological costs of having a relative with mental ill-ness may include embarrassment at the illness or at the behaviors of the person with mental illness, anger, depression, and finally, simply feeling overwhelmed by the intensity of the relative's needs (even when he or she refuses to accept help). This chapter examines psy-chological costs by kinship role, residence, and family burden.

WHAT IS SUBJECTIVE BURDEN?

The reader is reminded of the important distinction between ob-jective and subjective burden first noted more than three decades ago by Hoenig and Hamilton (1966). Possible costs of mental illness to family members involve more than time and money (Hatfield 1978; Thompson and Doll 1982; Lefley 1987b). The term *subjective burden* refers to the variety of stressful "psychological or emotional costs" of severe mental illness to family members (Hatfield 1978; Thompson and Doll 1982). These costs are incurred in terms of generalized emotional distress and are an important element of the family experience with mental illness. Recall that Chapters 3, 4, and 5 focused on *objective* family burden or what it is that family members *actually do* for their relative. We now turn to subjective burden or what it is that family members *feel*. In this chapter we seek to link experience in caregiving (objective burden) to emotional distress (subjective burden).

As an outcome, distress has a long history in studies of family burden, whether labeled as subjective burden, emotional costs, or psychological costs. From the family member and interviewer comments presented above, one might conclude that there are probably as many emotional costs related to the family experience with mental illness as there are family members. Yet there are common threads that run through various studies. As early as 1978, Agnes Hatfield, a researcher and family member, detailed the "psychological costs" of mental illness to family members (1978). She reported that 65 percent of a sample of 89 family members (almost 87 percent were parents) belonging to a support group for relatives of persons with schizophrenia reported unspecified stress because of the illness. Other areas of emotional burden that were reported were anxiety (30%), resentment (24%), and grief and depression (22%).

Early research also utilized the concept of "emotional costs" to summarize the typical painful reactions that family members may experience in caring for a relative with chronic mental illness (Thompson and Doll 1982). The authors reported that 46 percent of a random sample of the relatives of postdischarge "patients" reported feelings of embarrassment (p. 383). Others have noted that family reactions to the illness of a relative include anger, shame, and grief (Cook 1988; Lefley 1989; Schene 1990).

Another model portrays emotional costs as a set of discrete stages, with the first stage consisting of feelings of "uneasiness and a need for reassurance," which progresses to anger through shame and then to grief (Raymond, Slaby, and Lieb 1975). Family members such as Carol Howe, the mother of two sons with schizophrenia, have spoken of the typical reactions expressed in support groups: "Generally, the first time a family comes to a support meeting there is a tremendous catharsis in being able to share—often for the very first time—the pain and grief, the frustration and the anger about the illness of their relative" (American Orthopsychiatric Association 1987, 6).

To summarize, family members may experience strong feelings when faced with mental illness, and it is their emotional responses that are the object of explanation in this chapter. We will focus on feelings of embarrassment (distinguishing between those arising from the mental illness and those arising from the behaviors of the ill person), anger, depression, and simply feeling overwhelmed by the intensity of the consumer's needs. We call this variable Emotional Distress.

FACTORS RELATED TO EMOTIONAL DISTRESS

In the analyses to follow, we seek to link experience in caregiving to emotional distress, and to examine whether males and females react differently to varying types of caregiving. Whatever direct effects the sex of those studied has on emotional distress, it may also condition the effects of other factors. We were especially interested in how men and women react to two distinct dimensions of caregiving: Care and Control (see Chapters 3 and 4).

Recall that Care refers to helping the patient with such activities of daily living as preparing meals, getting dressed, doing the laundry, and other household chores. Control refers to efforts to manage embarrassing or threatening behaviors, night disturbances, and substance abuse, among other troublesome behaviors. Since the former tasks are stereotypically female, and the latter stereotypically male, it is likely that males will be more distressed by having to provide Care around activities of daily living, whereas females will be more distressed by the need to Control behavioral problems.

Insofar as personal identity is structured by sex roles, role strain can be expected to occur when there is a conflict between the previously held definition of a sex role linked to a family role and the new added obligations of caregiving to a dependent adult. Addition of the caregiving or supervisory role may strain the existing role relationship particularly if the new obligations are perceived as incongruent with one's own gender identity. The more responsibilities are added that go beyond what is believed appropriate to a relationship with an adult son, daughter, brother, sister, or other relative, the more that emotional distress will be associated with performance of the role.

The family of orientation is particularly vulnerable to psychological distress, with parents experiencing ambivalent emotions. On the one hand there may be grief and depression from feelings of loss both for themselves and for their adult sons and daughters. At the same time, there may be feelings of anger and of being unfairly burdened. In a study of grief and depressive symptoms using a sample composed largely of parents and siblings, the authors reported that caregivers' distress was equal to that of a sample of homeless men and women in public shelters, and higher than that of persons with multiple sclerosis (Struening et al. 1995).

Although research on the effect of mental illness on siblings has long been neglected, siblings may feel embarrassed by the illness itself as well as by the behaviors of their brother or sister, and angry about the attention that the ill family member receives (Johnson 1990). Spouses may feel anger when the other spouse is not able to keep up his or her share of family responsibilities. Adult children of parents with mental illness have typically grown up with the knowledge that mental illness has interfered with their mothers' and fathers' parental roles. We know little about the emotional costs to more secondary relatives.

Some of the signs and symptoms of mental illness are likely to have adverse affects on all members of the family, regardless of their family role and gender. Symptoms that confuse or frighten, or are in other ways unfamiliar, tend to distress all members of the family. However, there is also variability in response, and different family members may also respond to the signs and symptoms of mental illness in different ways, depending on their attitudes toward mental illness.

Lefley (1989) has suggested that the stigma of mental illness generalizes from the consumer of mental health services to other family members. Hence the stigma arising from the mental illness of a relative may be expected to have a variety of adverse effects, coloring family interactions within the family. Stigma is a negative outcome closely related to burden. Where there is a history of felt stigma, we anticipate that there is also more current emotional distress (Clausen 1981; Lefley 1989).

There is, however, a countervailing process that may offset the negative effects of illness severity and stigma. This is client contributions to the family household, which, as a source of positive feelings, will tend to offset other negative feelings. As we will see in Chapter 8, mental illness does not necessarily rule out reciprocal exchanges between patients and their families, such as helping with meal preparation, shopping, or other household chores; giving financial assistance; listening to problems and offering advice; giving news about mutual friends and family; and providing companionship. To the extent that consumers can fulfill some familial obligations, and such exchanges do occur, they are predicted to offset some of the emotional distress that family members experience in response to the illness (Stoneall 1983).

MEASURES

The results presented in this chapter use data from the third (final) wave of interviews. At this time the items that make up Emotional Distress were added to the structured interview. The items were asked only of the 282 (out of 305) family members who had contact with the consumer during the last year.

The measure of Emotional Distress was developed by the authors in collaboration with Dr. Gene Fisher of the Social and Demographic Research Institute. Items include the family member's anger, depression, and embarrassment because of the mental illness or the client's behavior. A final global item asks for the respondent's perception of being overwhelmed by the intensity of the consumer's need for family care. The specific statements are: I am very angry with my relative; I get depressed when I think about my relative; My relative's behavior embarrasses me; My relative's illness is an embarrassment to me; and, Taking care of my relative is a heavier burden than I can bear. Response categories and their coding are: strongly disagree = 1, disagree = 2, ambivalent = 3, agree = 4, and strongly agree = 5. Thus, higher scores reflect more subjective distress.

The third wave of family interviews also included questions about stigma felt since the onset of the relative's mental illness. Experiences since onset were used as a window for response because stigma may be felt keenly early in the history of the illness, and then overcome. Thus, a 30-day time frame would miss some significant expressions of the stigma as experienced by family members. The items include worry about: people finding out about the illness, neighbors treating them differently, friends and neighbors avoiding them, and being treated differently by even their best friends. Other items inquire about the need to hide the illness or keep it a secret, the avoidance of social events, not seeing friends, and feelings of shame or embarrassment. The measurement of stigma employs a dichotomous yes-no format for response. The "yes-no" categories for response were chosen to simplify the respondent's last task (stigma items occur at the end of the interview).

Table 6.1
Frequency of Emotional Distress

Statement	% Agree or Strongly Agree
I get depressed when I think about my relative.	33.0
My relative's behavior embarrasses me.	20.3
Taking care of my relative is a heavier burden than I can bear.	17.0
My relative's illness is an embarrassment to me.	14.2
I am very angry with my relative.	10.1

Notes: Response categories: strongly disagree = 1; disagree = 2; ambivalent = 3; agree = 4; and strongly agree = 5.

Other measures included in the analyses at T3 consist of family reports of patient contributions to the household (Reciprocity), patient reports of symptom frequency (Symptoms), and psychiatric diagnosis based on medical records (Schizophrenia compared with other diagnoses). The measures of assistance with daily living (Care) and supervision of behavior problems (Control) are the same as those presented in Chapters 3 and 4.

RESULTS

As we turn to the results, the reader is reminded that the client sample consisted of slightly more males (53 percent) than females. The average client was 33 years old and had 11.5 years of education. A majority (61%) of the clients had received a diagnosis of schizophrenia. For three out of four clients, the onset of the illness was late adolescence or early adulthood (median age = 20 years).

We begin with the prevalence of emotional distress. A total of 80 percent of the respondents acknowledged at least some emotional distress. Table 6.1 shows that depression was the emotion reported most frequently. Almost a third of the respondents agreed or agreed strongly that they get depressed when they think about the patient. Just over a fifth reported being embarrassed by the patient's behavior. Approximately 17 percent felt overwhelmed by caretaking responsibilities and agreed that taking care of the consumer represented a heavier burden than they could bear. Fourteen percent agreed that they were embarrassed by the illness. About 10 percent agreed that they felt very angry with the patient.

However, a group of 33 family members expressed no emotional cost whatsoever. These family members *strongly disagreed* with all five statements. When emotional response is viewed as a summary scale, the mean is 2.2 (closer to disagreeing with the statements than to ambivalent feelings) on a scale of 1 (strongly disagree) to 5 (strongly agree). Once again we see that family experiences vary considerably, with some relatives relating extraordinary emotional costs and others reporting very little negative price.

Analyses of the relationship between family role, living arrangements, and emotional distress produced only marginally significant results, but the basic patterns are noteworthy. In terms of intensity of emotional distress, the following results were obtained: adult children scored the lowest (1.92), followed by other relatives (2.18), siblings (2.23), parents (2.26), and finally, spouses, who scored the highest (2.30). In addition, family members who *did not live* with the consumer at the time of the interview reported more emotional distress than family members who were currently living with the consumer (2.25 versus 1.11). The lower distress experienced by co-resident family members may explain why they were willing to invite the relative with mental illness to live with them, rather than reflecting a salutatory effect of co-residence per se. Family members who experience high levels of emotional distress associated with their relative's behavioral problems are probably less willing to enter into, or to continue, a shared living arrangement.

Our final model presents a multivariate analysis in which we correct for intrafamily clustering and duplication of patient variables at the family level of analysis. Our results support the gender-role hypothesis, showing that the *direct* effect of gender is very small indeed.

As Table 6.2 indicates, there is evidence of significant direct effects of symptoms, diagnosis, stigma, and reciprocity. That is, emotional distress is increased for family members who have experienced more stigma, whose relatives report more symptoms, and when the relative has also received a diagnosis of schizophrenia. As predicted, emotional distress is reduced as the consumer plays a reciprocal role in family life.

Table 6.2 also shows that the interactive differences between male and female effects on distress are statistically significant. Care is as-

Table 6.2
Predicting Emotional Distress: Specified Effects Model (N = 269)

Variable	Metric Coefficient	Significance
Symptoms	.136	.008
Schizophrenia	.301	.001
Stigma	1.106	.000
Reciprocity	-.285	.000
Respondent = Female	.098	.306
Care* Female	-.658	.021
Care* Male	1.111	.050
Control* Female	3.430	.000
Control* Male	.435	.650
Adjusted R²	.405	

Notes: Huber variance estimates are used to adjust for the duplication of patient characteristics across multiple respondents. The method of estimation is least squares, but the standard errors have been adjusted to account for cluster sampling. The estimated coefficients are unchanged from ordinary least squares regression.

sociated with less distress for females and more distress for males. Control makes no difference for males, but is a major predictor of distress among females.

DISCUSSION

As stays in psychiatric hospitals have declined in length, it is more and more often women who are left "mothering the chronically mentally ill," presumably because they feel more responsible (Cook 1988). In fact, most observers believe that the burden of adult mental illness falls more heavily on females than on males (Biegel, Sales, and Schulz 1991; Fisher, Benson, and Tessler 1990). But the literature focuses on mothers as distinct from other relationships, and men are compared only rarely. Hence, our sample of both men and women who had a variety of relations with the mentally ill person including mother, father, husband, wife, brother, sister, son, and daughter, as well as other secondary kin relationships such as grandmother, grandfather, aunt, and uncle offered an excellent opportunity to examine gender issues with respect to family role and burden.

In fact, the stress of *caregiving* does vary by sex, but the effects are conditioned by the nature of the caregiving. If Care issues are paramount, males tend to be more adversely affected. But when Control issues are active, females tend to be most distressed. These results carry interesting implications for the different needs of male and female caregivers for supportive services. Thus, for example, access to homemaker aides may be a necessary adjunct service when the primary caregiver is male, whereas access to 24-hour crisis intervention may be a higher priority when the primary caregiver is female. Overall, when caregiving tasks are felt to be gender appropriate, family members tend not to be highly distressed.

There are many sources of distress for family members of relatives with mental illness, in addition to Care and Control. As we have seen, the stigma that family members feel, the intensity of the symptoms their relative exhibits, as well as diagnosis, tend to affect both male and female members of the family in the same adverse way. These negative effects can be mitigated, to some extent, depending on what the relative with mental illness is able and willing to do in return. Thus, keeping the psychological costs of caregiving reined in appears to be a matter of reciprocity between the relative with mental illness and his or her family caregivers.

Maintaining social relationships of any depth can be expected to be problematic, and the more severe the mental disorder, the more fragile the relationship. Without concerted attention to the family caregivers' emotional distress arising out of the patients' illness, as well as caregiving experiences, it is all too likely that some kinship obligations may wither and that persons with mental illness will be left to depend on what the public system of care is able and willing to provide.

Chapter 7

What Were the Positive Aspects for Family Members?

A major dilemma facing family caregivers is to how to nurture positive aspects of the relationship and keep alive warm family feelings toward a relative when faced with the stigma, behavioral problems, and caregiving burdens that mental disorder may bring in its wake (Stoneall 1983). The discord, tension, and disappointment that follows the recognition of mental illness can be so intense that family members fail to see any benefits or gratifications at all from their relationship with the consumer.

However, having a relative with mental illness may not rule out the possibility that family members may experience some personal benefits (Greenberg, Seltzer, and Greenley 1993). Among the potential benefits to be experienced are client contributions to the family household and other personal gratifications that may emerge out of the relationship. In this chapter, we explore benefits and gratifications as part of the total family experience. Research in this area is still quite new and also somewhat controversial among members of organized family groups who worry that highlighting the potential rewards associated with mental illness may provide a pretext for the mental health system to increase the burden on families.

GRATIFICATIONS

Early professional views of the quality of the relations between family members and consumers defined the relationship as problematic, with parents in particular blamed as the cause of mental illness. Even now when family members are viewed as reactors to the illness or partners in treatment, little research has been devoted to the positive attitudes of family members, although these caring attitudes represent one important source of gratification for family members and consumers.

Until the 1990s, one searched the literature in vain to answer the question: Is there anything positive? More typically, research on the relationships between family members and consumers has described the "rejecting of the patient" by family members (Kreisman, Simmens, and Joy 1979). Much of the expressed emotion literature focuses on the relationship between the hostile and critical attitudes of family members and the relapse and rehospitalization of the consumer (Leff and Vaughn 1985; Fisher, Benson, and Tessler 1990).

However, researchers recently have begun to report the positive along with the negative side of family experiences with mental illness. One study compared both the gratifications and frustrations of aging mothers of adult offspring with mental illness with mothers of adult children with mental retardation (Greenberg, Seltzer, and Greenley 1993). Using measures taken from the gerontology literature, the authors reported that mothers whose adult children had mental illness reported more frustrations and fewer gratifications than did the group of mothers of adults with mental retardation when residence was shared (548).

Bulger and colleagues (1993) studied both the burdens and gratifications experienced by parents of sons and daughters with schizophrenia. A sample of 60 parents reported many gratifications, including feeling closer to their adult child, happiness that the family was providing care, increased self-esteem, and insights into personal strengths. No parent reported having no gratifications. Very little caregiver burden was reported, and gratifications were not associated with levels of objective burden.

Another approach was taken by Horwitz and his colleagues (1996), who studied reciprocal exchanges between 66 family members and their relatives with serious mental illness. Family members' provision of caregiving and support was the best predictor of contributions by consumers. The authors concluded that the norm of reciprocity still operates in this family situation, although it need not involve equivalent exchanges.

In 1997, a cross-cultural approach reported that the cultural norm of providing care for elderly parents is a major motivation for Japanese caregivers (Yamamoto and Wallhagen 1997). However, the authors note that although female caregivers found value in their filial piety, it "should not be used as a reason for policies that are unduly restrictive to the lifestyle choices of those individuals whose elderly parents happen to be afflicted by physical or cognitive impairments" (175).

In this chapter, the dependent variable is a measure of the gratifications that the family member derives from the relationship. We conceptualize these gratifications as the warm emotions that family members feel toward the consumer, including enjoying being with him or her, loving him or her, feeling that he or she is an important part of the family member's life, being happy to do things for him or her, and feeling that he or she makes the family member happy. Interviewers asked family members: People who have (relatives/friends) with mental health problems often have mixed feelings about them. As I read each of the following statements, tell me how you feel about your relative right now. Do you strongly agree (coded 5), agree (coded 4), feel ambivalent (coded 3), disagree (coded 2), or strongly disagree (coded 1) with what these statements say about your relative? An example of a statement is: It makes me happy to do things for my relative. The scale has a reliability coefficient of .870 (Cronbach's alpha).

Several factors can affect whether a family member experiences his or her relationship with the consumer as gratifying. Below we develop the rationales for predicting gratifications based on whether consumers make a reciprocal contribution to the family (contributions), whether family members accept the sick role associated with mental illness (attribution), and whether family members have experienced stigmatization (stigma). Accordingly, the next sections consider in turn some factors likely to affect the attitudes of family members toward the consumer of mental health services.

CONTRIBUTIONS

Even when the sick role associated with serious mental illness is accepted, adult family relationships imply some expectation of reciprocity. Goode (1960) has suggested that if, *for whatever reason*, a person fails to fulfill family role obligations, the resulting strain in the role set may evoke a punishing response. But even though mental illness may be disabling in certain ways, such as restricting educational attainment and occupational performance, it does not necessarily rule out all reciprocal exchanges between consumers and their families (Horwitz, Reinhard, and Howell-White 1996).

Reciprocity may be both instrumental and expressive. As we have noted before, research language tends to ignore the fact that the consumer is a family member, too, and as such may give help with household chores, offer a sympathetic ear, or, quite importantly, provide companionship. To the extent that such client contributions do occur, they may offset some of the other problems that are present (see Chapter 7). Our current hypothesis is that the greater the level of client contributions to the family member respondent, the more the relationship will be seen as gratifying.

In fact, client contributions to their families may be quite substantial, according to a study of 725 families living in Wisconsin (Greenberg, Greenley, and Benedict 1994). Almost 60 percent of family members reported that they received companionship from the consumer. From 50 to 80 percent of persons with severe mental illness who lived with their family members made some contribution to the household such as helping with chores or listening to problems.

Our measure of client contributions is derived from the National Survey of Families and Households (Sweet, Bumpass, and Call 1988). The measure describes what, if anything, the consumer did to benefit the family member during the previous 30 days. The items include: helping with meal preparation, shopping, or other household chores; giving financial assistance; listening to problems and offering advice; giving news about mutual friends and family; and providing companionship. The scale has a reliability coefficient of .745 (Cronbach's alpha).

ATTRIBUTION

Having a family member with a chronic and long-term illness means to some extent acceptance of the sick role by both the FM and the RMI. If a family member is legitimately defined as sick in our society, he or she is relieved to some degree of the rights and obligations of normative adult roles. David Landy, working within the Parsonian model, has noted that the acceptance of the sick role by persons with physical illnesses requires the adoption of a "dependent childlike status" (Landy 1977). The adoption of the dependent role and other behavioral aspects of serious mental illness may lead to various attributions by family members as to the true nature of the malady from which the consumer suffers.

A diagnosed mental disorder is not always defined as an illness by family members, and we have noted the importance of attribution in previous chapters. The consumer's behaviors may be attributed to a personality defect, a moral failing, a supernatural basis, a lack of motivation, a physical injury, or the abuse of drugs or alcohol rather than as the symptoms of a *real* illness. The more that troublesome and burdensome behaviors are seen as under the consumer's control, the less likely family members will be to accept behaviors as symptoms of an illness, and the less likely they will be to have positive feelings of warmth and affection.

Recall that the attribution measure asked family members to state how much they believed six statements were true. Each suggested that the client's behaviors and symptoms were under his or her control—contrary to a sick role attribution, which views troublesome behaviors as symptoms of illness and, as such, outside of the client's control. Examples include, "My relative could have controlled some of his or her difficult behavior if she had really wanted," and "My relative didn't try hard enough to get better." We reasoned that agreement with the six statements would signify acceptance of the sick role, and hypothesized that sick role attributions would be associated with reporting more gratifications from the relationship.

STIGMA

The stigma of mental illness creates a special dilemma for family members who may be distressed by the stigma that is directed toward their relative with mental illness. But in addition to the stigma felt by the consumer, "stigma also generalizes to their families" (Lefley 1989). When a family member feels stigma, it may negatively affect feelings toward the member with mental illness who is seen as the stigma's source. "Since a close relationship results in being 'tainted' oneself a relative can choose either to embrace the fate of the stigmatized person and identify with him or to reject sharing the discredit of the stigmatized person by avoiding or terminating the relationship" (Kreisman and Joy 1974, 39). Most members of the sample had chosen the former path, as is implied by their agreeing to three interviews.

The stigma items we administered to family members consisted of such statements as, "You worried whether people would find out about the consumer's condition?" and "You kept the consumer's illness a secret?" Using the same items as in the previous chapter, we showed that when family members feel stigma associated with having a relative with mental illness, they tend to experience heightened emotional distress. In the current chapter we test the hypothesis that feeling stigmatized negatively affects family member attitudes toward the relative with mental illness. In theory, this would occur whether stigma is perceived as directed at the client or as generalizing to the family.

FAMILY ROLE AND RESIDENCE

In this chapter we compare parents with other family members in terms of the gratifications derived from the relationships with the consumer. Although parents have been a focus of at least some research on gratifications (Bulger, Wandersman, and Goldman 1993), there clearly is a need to expand the analysis of gratifications to include a variety of kinship relations.

Since the ties between parents and children are perhaps the strongest of all bonds, parents may be expected to hold more positive attitudes than adult children, spouses, siblings, or other family members. Nonparental family roles would appear to be much more tenuous in the face of prolonged dependency because of mental illness. Parenting, according to some observers, is a lifelong role that cannot be outgrown or ended capriciously (Cook and Cohler 1986).

Intuitively we would expect family members who share a residence with the consumer of mental health services to have positive feelings toward him or her. If the family member were not positively disposed, he or she might make a different residential choice. But co-residence also tends to magnify disability and stigma and to increase objective burden. Thus, how if at all co-residence will be related to gratifications needs to be explored.

ILLNESS CHARACTERISTICS

No analysis of factors affecting relationship gratification would be complete without controlling for the severity of the diagnosis and the duration of the illness. By all accounts the nature and history of the illness is at the core of the family experience. Diagnoses of schizophrenia, in particular, appears to compromise relations with kin. How illness history affects family members is less clear. A longer period of illness may give family members more opportunity to accept the illness and disability. As consumers age, some of the more florid symptoms also tend to abate, and improvement in the clinical condition may actually occur (Harding et al. 1987). However, aging mothers of adult sons and daughters with mental illness may have fewer resources and are more likely to be widowed (Greenberg et al. 1993). Longer exposure to discord caused by the illness may wear out the patience of aging family members, leaving a residue of frustration (Cook et al. 1994).

OTHER RELATED FACTORS

Previous research has not to any great extent found associations between caregiving burden and demographic variables (Fisher, Benson, and Tessler 1990). Since the picture might differ with respect to gratifications, we explored a variety of possible relationships of demographic variables to gratifications. However, we found substantially the same results. Neither client or family member age were significantly associated with gratifications. Consistent with other burden research, income was also not a significant correlate of gratifications. Objective burden (Care and Control) was also random with respect to gratifications. The sex of the respondents did not make a difference; there was no difference between male family members and female family members with respect to positive feelings, nor was there a difference in how they felt about male and female consumers. Only one demographic variable, race, was statistically significant. Black family members were more likely than white family members to report that their relationships with the relative with mental illness were gratifying.

In thinking about race differences in gratifications, it is useful to note recent findings suggesting that black parents bear adversity better than white parents (Pickett et al. 1993). Pickett and colleagues suggest that "this does not minimize the pain parents experience as a result of their offspring's mental illness, but instead shows an acceptance of the illness as a problem like any other in life, to be managed accordingly" (464). The accepting attitude of black kin is likely to lead to more positive feelings about the relationship compared with what the authors call the "abstracted normative developmental expectations" of white family members.

RESEARCH APPROACH

The tables and discussion that follow address two distinct but related issues: First, is there anything positive?, and second, what factors make it more (or less) likely that the relationship will be experienced in a gratifying way? The 30-day time frame, used as a framework in the burden chapters, is less relevant in these analyses. Gratifications, stigma, and attributions are conceptualized as producing strongly held attitudes that do not fit as well within a 30-day framework. We also note that the data for the analyses to follow are drawn from the T3 (1992) interviews because some of the crucial measures were included only at T3. As much as possible, we present individual items in the tables so that the reader can clearly see what is included in a multi-item scale.

The exposition begins with simple tabulations and cross-tabulations, and then moves to a multivariate analysis that is designed to bring together the various factors affecting gratifications. The final equation models gratifications as a function of: client contributions, stigma, and attributions indicating the use of an illness model. We will test these effects simultaneously, controlling for severity of diagnosis and duration of illness, family role (parent), residence, and race.

RESULTS

As is reported in Table 7.1, family members experience a great deal of gratification from their relationships with their relatives with mental illness. Approximately 93 percent agreed that they love the consumer very much. A large majority of family members report that it makes them happy to do things for the client (82%); that they enjoy being with the client (78%); and that the consumer is an important part of their life (78%). We see the most ambivalence around the statement, "The consumer makes me happy" (only 70% agreed). Overall, family members averaged close to agree or strongly agree with all items. The mean is 3.92 and Cronbach's alpha is .870.

There are significant differences among family members in how much gratification they experience in relation to their relative with

Table 7.1
Frequency of Positive Feelings

Statement	% Agree or Strongly Agree
I love him or her very much.	92.6
It makes me happy to do things for him or her.	81.5
I enjoy being with him or her.	78.1
He or she is an important part of my life.	77.7
He or she makes me happy.	70.1
% averaging agree or strongly agree with all statements	62.9

mental illness. Adult children (4.179) unexpectedly scored the highest on the gratifications scale, followed by parents (4.096), spouses (3.825), siblings (3.811), and other kin (3.721).

Table 7.2 shows the extent and kinds of client contributions that may be interpreted as benefiting family members, with the items rank-ordered in terms of prevalence. Slightly more than half reported receiving companionship and slightly less than half received news about friends and family. Instrumental helping was less frequent but still present for 13 to 21 percent of the family members who reported receiving help with meals, shopping, household chores, or financial assistance. A majority of family members (64%) reported some benefit. Those who did benefit (n = 194) reported benefits in more than two areas (average = 2.56).

The frequency of stigma is shown in Table 7.3. Unexpectedly, family members did not report a high level of stigma. Only one-fifth of family members answered positively to two or more of the stigma items. This is remarkable when we remember that family members were asked, "Was there ever a time when . . . ," and thus these are estimates of stigma perceived over the course of the illness.

Approximately 20 percent reported avoiding going to large parties with the client, and about another fifth worried that people would find out about the condition. About 16 percent reported that they didn't see friends as often as before. About 8 percent worried that neighbors would treat them differently or that friends and neighbors would avoid them. Only 4 percent worried that their best friends would treat them differently.

Table 7.2
Frequency of Client Contributions to Family

In the past 30 days my relative...	%
gave me companionship.	50.8
gave me news about friends and family.	48.2
listened to my problems and offered advice.	29.5
helped me with meals, shopping or chores.	20.7
gave me financial assistance.	13.4
Total (at least one area)	63.6
....	....
Total (mean # of areas, n = 305)	1.63
Total (mean # of areas, n = 194)	2.56

Note: The mean number of areas is shown below the dotted line, first for the total sample and then for those who received at least some benefit.

Table 7.3
Frequency of Stigma

Statement	% Yes
You avoided going to large parties or social events with your relative.	19.5
You worried whether people would find out about your relative's condition.	18.8
You didn't see some of your friends as often as you did before.	15.6
You sometimes felt the need to hide your relative's illness.	12.9
You kept your relative's illness a secret.	11.9
You worried that your neighbors would treat you differently.	8.3
You worried that friends and neighbors would avoid you after they found out about it.	8.0
You worried that even your best friends would treat you differently.	3.7
Total Responding Yes to 2 or More of 8 Items	21.1

Table 7.4 reports the responses of family members to the attribution items. Recall that attribution as used here represents an illness model as an explanation of the client's problems. The illness model implies that the client has no voluntary control over behaviors that presumably are seen as symptoms of the illness.

Table 7.4
Family Attributions of Mental Illness

Statement	% *Not* True
My relative had these problems because of a weak personality.	66.2
My relative didn't try hard enough to get better.	62.3
My relative could make strange thoughts and feelings come and go at will.	55.1
My relative could have controlled *most* of his or her difficult behavior if he or she had really wanted.	54.8
My relative could have participated more in family activities if he or she had really wanted.	44.3
My relative could have controlled *some* of his or her difficult behavior if he or she had really wanted.	38.0

As many as two-thirds did not believe that the client's problems were because of a weak personality. Just less than two-thirds (62%) felt that the consumer was in fact trying hard enough to get better (or alternately that the statement didn't apply because it was a real illness and not responsive to voluntary control). A majority rejected the notion that the client could have controlled *most* of his or her difficult behaviors if he or she had really wanted. However, somewhat fewer (38%) believed that he or she could control *some* difficult behaviors if he or she really wanted. More than half rejected the idea that the client could make strange thoughts and feelings come and go at will. However, more than half (56%) believed that the client could have participated more in family activities if he or she had wanted to.

Table 7.5 reports the results of a statistical analysis that allows us to show the effects on gratifications of being black, being a parent, living with the RMI, the number of years the relative has been ill, a diagnosis of schizophrenia, client contributions, stigma, and accepting that the RMI has a sickness. As shown the model explains almost one-third of the variability in FM gratifications scores.

Of the demographic variables (age, sex, income, marital status, and education, and client sex and age) that were measured, only ethnicity predicted gratifications. As predicted, black family members experienced significantly more relational gratifications than white family members. The results also show that parents tend to experience more

Table 7.5
Predicting Gratifications (N = 270)

Variable	Coefficient
Ethnicity (1 = black)	.331** (3.470)
Family Role (1 = parent)	.206** (2.640)
Residence (1 = co-residence)	-.404** (-3.339)
Years Ill (in years)	-.014* (-2.516)
Diagnosis (1 = schizophrenia)	-.220* (-2.155)
Client Contributions (mean)	.422*** (8.244)
Stigma (mean)	-.551** (-2.753)
Sick Role Attribution (mean)	.162** (3.098)
Adjusted R^2 = .316	

Notes: ***p <.001; **p <.01; *p <.05
Huber variance estimates are used to adjust for the duplication of patient characteristics across multiple respondents. The methods of estimation is least squares, but
the standard errors have been adjusted to account for cluster sampling. The estimated coefficients are unchanged.

gratifications when compared with adult children, spouses, siblings,
and other secondary kin *as a group*. The positive effect of being a
parent on felt gratifications is independent of whether sons and
daughters are living with them. The effect of co-residence, to our
surprise, was negative. That is, living together was associated with
significantly fewer gratifications.

Table 7.5 also shows the impact of the clients' clinical condition
in terms of *years ill* and *diagnosis*. As expected, both duration and a
diagnosis of schizophrenia predict fewer relational gratifications. Also
as predicted, when the relative with mental illness is viewed as contributing to the relationship, family members tend to experience these
relationships as more gratifying. Of all the independent variables included in the model, client contributions is far and away the strongest
predictor. However, stigma also makes an important contribution to
the prediction of gratification, notwithstanding the finding that
stigma is more the exception than the rule. When stigma is present,
it has a negative effect on warm feelings toward the consumer. Finally, gratifications are also structured by how family members per-

ceive the illness and whether they believe that the client (or the illness) is in control. When problem behaviors and symptoms are seen as beyond the control of the client, feelings toward the client are more positive.

DISCUSSION

The main objective of this chapter was to answer the question, Is there anything positive? Secondarily, we were interested in identifying factors that increase (or decrease) the likelihood of gratifications. On both counts, the results reported are encouraging.

When family members are asked about positive feelings toward their relative with mental illness, they report far more gratifications than the family burden literature suggests. To be sure, we find this for family members who choose to remain involved (and who are presumably most burdened), but even for them the impression is one of positive feelings about the relationship. One could also see duty, responsibility, or resignation motivating such involvement. But at least part of the motivation appears to be positive and anchored in loving feelings toward the consumer of mental health services. We also see that as in any relationship, love does not always equate with happiness. More family respondents stated that they love the consumer very much than stated that he or she makes them happy.

The accepting attitude of black kin indeed is associated with more positive feelings about the relationship compared with white family members. Although the data are not shown, this relationship still is significant even when controlling for income. Our results support the argument that because blacks may be exposed to more hassles on a daily basis (e.g., discrimination and violence), the mental illness of a relative per se may lose the importance that it otherwise holds if it is the primary negative event in a family member's life.

Although the subsample of adult children was relatively small (n = 19) we were surprised that their gratification scores were the highest. Given the concern about the negative effect that mental illness can have on fulfilling the parenting role, we might have expected to see signs of more troubled parent-child relationships. But at least in our subsample of adult children, this is not at all the case, as these offspring have very warm feelings toward their parents.

With the exception of adult children, parents report more gratifications than most other family members, despite being the most burdened (see Chapter 3). It is ironic that parents who have among the warmest feelings are most burdened. (Indeed, this may be why they are most burdened!) The strong commitments exhibited by parents are best interpreted in term of family structure and the norm of parental obligation.

We observed a negative effect of co-residence on gratifications, despite the fact that one might have reasoned that persons who choose to live together have very warm feelings toward one another. The negative effect may instead result from the discord, tension, and disappointment that tend to be most salient and frequent when people live under the same roof. The implication is that relationships between kin will be most gratifying if, when appropriate, the client can live independently of the family member. That we did not find a co-residence effect mitigates somewhat the "social desirability" argument (people will give the socially desirable response when interviewed, i.e., "Of course I love him or her") as an explanation for the large amounts of gratifications that family members reported.

Rather than the march of time leading to patterns of acceptance, a chronic illness seems to tax the relationship. It is the number of years since the consumer first received help for mental health problems that affects gratifications and not the client's age itself. The effect of the family member's aging process does not seem to be implicated, since family member age was not significantly associated with gratifications.

The results indicate that from the family perspective, stigma is an important predictor of relationship gratifications. Stigma was not reported in large amounts, but when it occured, it was of prime importance in affecting how family members felt about the relative with mental illness. When the stigma of mental illness appeared to have generalized to the family, members tended to experience few gratifications from the relationship with the relative with mental illness. Future research should examine whether the apparent success of family organizations in reducing feelings of stigma among their members is also associated with more positive feelings toward the person with mental illness.

The term *mental illness* is used with such frequency that we expected there to be shared understandings about what it means. Yet we have seen that the "illness" model is not entirely accepted by some family members. To the extent that an alternate explanation implying voluntary control by the consumer is used to account for the problematic behaviors and symptoms of mental illness, positive feelings toward the client are decreased. It should be noted that there is also a history of professional disagreement about the illness model of deviant behavior (Szasz 1961; Scheff 1984).

Instrumental and expressive contributions by clients to family members also represent a positive dimension of the family experience. When conceptualized as an independent variable, client contributions are the most important predictor of positive feelings toward the relative with mental illness. The emergence of the consumer movement and the trend for consumers to become more active participants in their own treatment are positive developments for most families. As consumers are empowered to leave the dependent role, they can be expected to take a more active role in family life. As a result, relations among kin may become more gratifying.

Mental health professionals can also do much to encourage clients to contribute to their families within the limits of their functional capabilities. Professionals need to remember that consumers are family members, too, and need to be supported in their family roles. The potential benefit to both families and consumers looms large.

Chapter 8

How Involved Were Other Members of the Family Household?

This chapter turns from our previous focus on individual family members toward the family *household* as the unit of analysis. What is the experience of household members other than the primary caregiver? These household members, although not necessarily burdened in the traditional sense, may nonetheless be involved with the consumer as a result of living in the caregiver's household. What is their level of involvement with the relative with mental illness?

Although it is the family household that defines the family experience, the household as a social unit has received limited research attention. We know very little about the households of caregiving family members and the potential involvement of other household members with the consumer of mental health services. The research presented here is a preliminary attempt to use the household level of analysis to broaden our understanding of the total *family* experience.

It is often reported that although many consumers currently live alone in apartments, hotels, boardinghouses with single room occupancies, or in supervised housing, at least a third "live with family" (Fisher et al. 1992). However, the phrase *"live with family"* describes many arrangements. Returning to the family of procreation after a period of inpatient care may mean a return to a spouse and minor children, to the adult children of a dissolved marriage or perhaps to a cohabiting relationship. Return to the family of origin may mean a return to aging parents, an extended family, or to a sibling's household. Other family members such as grandparents, aunts, and uncles, as well as familylike "fictive kin"—such as significant others—may also play a role in the consumer's living arrangements. Such shared residences may foster the greater involvement of family members with consumers even though involvement does not require that family members live together.

Except for Chapter 7, which examined positive aspects of the family experience, previous chapters have drawn on the concept of "family burden" to describe the family experience. But the term *caregiver burden* would actually have been more appropriate, since it was the experiences of individuals, and not the family as a whole, that were addressed. An understanding of the total family experience with mental illness should include more than the burden of caregivers. Other family members, although not necessarily caregivers in the traditional sense, may nonetheless be as involved with their relative with a mental illness as they would with any relative. We tend to forget that in the role of family member, the person with mental illness interacts with a whole range of other family members.

Our knowledge of the involvement of relatives, other than primary caregivers, is quite limited. In 1971, Erving Goffman suggested that "it is not that the family finds that home life is made unpleasant" by a person with mental illness (366). But Cockerham's response to this conjecture suggests it is that the connections among family members are more tenuous than previously realized and the symptoms of mental illness may "distort and destroy the very core" (that is, love, affection, respect, loyalty, and responsibility) on which family involvement is based (1992, 217).

The view of the consumer as a "patient" with little expectation of adult autonomy led researchers to concentrate on the co-residential parental family of origin as potentially the most burdened. Siblings and the family of procreation have only recently become a focus of interest (Horwitz et al. 1992; Nicholson et al. 1993; Gamache, Tessler, and Nicholson 1995). Of particular concern is the potential involvement of minor children when the consumer continues to live in the household of the family of origin or establishes a family of procreation (Mapp 1994).

Harriet Lefley has noted the special vulnerability of both younger and older family members, asserting that "the negative impact of the patient's behavior on other family members, particularly children and adolescents, is an ongoing concern . . . ," and she has also eloquently pointed out the dilemma of aging parents (Lefley 1987, 1989a). Thus, members of extended families may be particularly vulnerable when households include either the grandchildren or grandparents of persons with mental illness.

In this chapter our research questions go beyond individual caregiving respondents to include the potential involvement of all members living in the households of the family members that consumers count on from time to time, whether or not the relative with mental illness is currently in residence. We begin by exploring basic descriptive questions about the members of the households of relatives chosen by consumers as involved in their daily lives. Who are the members that make up the households of persons named by consumers? How deeply are other individual household members involved with the user of mental health services? What is the distribution of minor children and elder adults as members of these households? How do caregiving respondents perceive the involvement of their younger and older household members compared with less vulnerable members?

We then turn to the households and ask: What are the family types and sizes of the households as a unit? How many households consist of the typically reported co-resident situations of parent/adult consumer family type? What other family types are represented? How does reported involvement with the consumer vary among households rather than among individual members? We conclude with a multivariate analysis that models involvement for both individual household members and households as a unit.

MEASURES

Most of our household measures come from the first section of the interview protocol administered to family members at all three interviews. This module enumerated the size and composition of the *respondent's* household, including whether or not the consumer was currently a member of that household. Each respondent was asked if the consumer lived in his or her home and for the total number of people living in the household. For each household member, the following variables were measured: sex, age, relationship to the former patient, and level of involvement.

Since both the individual household member and the household as a unit were of interest, a brief discussion of measurement is presented to help clarify the analyses. Some variables will change depending upon the unit of analysis. The following is an example: When the variable is age, the values for the household member analysis are the individuals' ages in years, but for the household unit of analysis, the values are the averages of the ages of all the household members. The household member analysis for four individuals as part of a household unit would use the values of their individual ages, such as 2, 8, 30, and 32. The household unit analysis would use the average value of 18 as a summary measure of household age.

Two important measures are involvement and family type. Level of involvement, the *dependent* variable in our multivariate analyses, is based on an item that asked the respondent family member to answer for himself or herself as well as for each household member "how deeply (he or she) was involved" with the consumer. If family members questioned what "involved" meant, they were told, "whatever it means to you." Response categories were coded such that: 0 equals not involved; 1 equals slightly involved; 2 equals somewhat involved; and 3 equals very involved.

To distinguish different family types, we assigned a numerical code to each household based on the relationships of household members *to the relative with mental illness*. The following six different family types were coded: (1) Extended Family (one or more parents and/or siblings *and* the consumer's spouse, children, or grandchildren); (2) Family of Origin (one or more natural or adoptive parents but no relatives of the marital family); (3) Family of Procreation (consumer's spouse and/or minor or adult children, foster children and/or grandchildren, but no member of the family of origin); (4) Independent Sibling Family (sibling and/or sibling-spouses and/or children and/or others but not the consumer's parents); (5) Fictive Kin Family (friends, acquaintances, significant others, roommates, foster parents, or ex-spouse; step- and in-law-only households); and (6) Secondary Kin Family (aunts, uncles, grandparents, cousins, nieces, etc.).

RESULTS

As Table 8.1 shows, the households of the 305 family respondents nominated by 175 consumers contained a total of 1,018 persons living in 279 unduplicated respondent households over the two years of the

Table 8.1
Households of Family Respondents

Residents	T1, T2, & T3	T1	T2	T3
Household Members (including consumers)	1018	869	797	787
Household Members (without consumers)	958	821	762	755
Household Members (co-resident)	197	168	160	131
Household Members (not co-resident)	761	653	602	624
Consumers (co-resident)	60	48	36	32
Consumers (not co-resident)	115	127	139	143

study. Thus, many more persons were potentially affected than the 305 persons actually interviewed.

Table 8.1 also shows the breakdown of household members and consumers by co-residence. Over the two years of the study, only 60 (out of 175) consumers were household members. Forty consumers lived in respondent households at Time 1, 36 at Time 2, and 32 at Time 3. Exits and entrances of other family members were related in a curvilinear way to whether and how many times during the two-year study period the consumer was co-resident. A stable pattern of consumer residence, that is, living in the household at all three points in time, was associated with the fewest exits and entrances of other household members. Also, if the consumer never lived in the household, there were relatively few exits and entrances. By far the most exits and entrances of other family members occurred when the consumer was in residence sporadically (that is, once or twice). House size averaged 2.8 persons, excluding the consumer, over the two years and ranged from one to eight members. Table 8.2 also reports the average involvement scores at Time 1 for household units by family type.

Consumer, family respondent, household member, and household unit characteristics are reported in Table 8.3. We repeat in this chap-

108   Family Experiences with Mental Illness

Table 8.2
Family Type and Household Member Involvement

Family Type	Household Members Include:	Involve-ment (mean)
Extended Family (n = 7)	One or more parents and/or siblings *and* the consumer's spouse, children or grandchildren	2.7
Family of Origin (n = 103)	One or more natural or adoptive parents but no relatives of the marital family	2.2
Family of Procreation (n = 32)	Consumer's spouse and/or minor or adult children, foster children and/or grandchildren	2.1
Independent Sibling Family (n = 66)	Sibling and/or sibling-spouses and/or children and/or others but not the consumer's parents	1.5
Fictive Kin Family (n = 31)	Friends, acquaintances, significant others, roommates, foster parents, or ex-spouse; step- and in-law only households	1.5
Secondary Kin Family (n = 39)	Aunts, uncles, grandparents, cousins, nieces, etc.	1.2

Notes: The variable Family Type was constructed by looking within each household at the relationships of household members to the consumer of mental health services. A one-way analysis of variance was significant (p = .000; f = 10.55; df = 5,272). The variable "Involvement" is coded such that: 0 = not involved; 1 = slightly involved; 2 = somewhat involved; and 3 = very involved.

ter descriptions of the family respondents and the consumers to highlight the comparisons we are making.

The consumer column shows the characteristics for the 175 consumers who nominated family members. There were slightly more males than females, and whites than blacks. The average consumer was 35.5 years old and had 11.5 years of education. Fifty-two percent had never been married. The most frequent diagnosis was that of schizophrenia (including schizoaffective disorder). Sixty-two percent were so diagnosed. Another 28 percent received a diagnosis of major depression or bipolar disorder. Approximately 43 percent of family members reported that the relative with mental illness had a case manager or helping team during the 12 months preceding the first family interview.

The family respondent column reports the descriptive statistics for the family respondents. Recall that the sample differed from many prior studies of the family experiences with mental illness in that

Table 8.3
Overview of Household Units

Variable	Consumer (N = 175)	Family Respondent (N = 305)	Household Member (N = 958)	Household Unit (N = 279)
Sex (% female)	46.9	70.8	52.3	54.9
Age (mean years)	35.5	50.6	31.4	37.5
Race (% black)	47.4[$]	48.5[&]	54.7	49.8
Education (mean years)	11.5	11.6	-	-
Marital Status (%)	52.0[#]	51.5[*]	53.3[#]	53.0[#]
Diagnosis (% schizophrenia)	62.1	63.9	62.2	63.5
Total Symptom Score (mean)	1.23	1.20	1.27	1.23
Continuous Case Management (%)	42.9	44.6	43.7	44.1
Consumer Has Children (% yes)	57.0	-	-	-
Low Income (% less than $10,000)	-	30.6	28.6	31.4
Parent	-	37.0	14.8	20.8[@]
Spouse	-	2.62	1.1	2.0[@]
Child	-	6.56	7.4	5.5[@]
Total House Size (mean w/o client)	-	2.83	3.5	2.8
Total Co-Residence	-	14.3	13.3	13.9
Total Involvement	-	2.0	1.62	1.7

Notes: [#]% consumer never married; [*]% family respondent currently married; [$]consumer race; [&]respondent race; [@]proportion of parent, spouse, or child within a household unit.

multiple family members were interviewed for slightly more than half of the consumers, and the sampling frame was not limited to primary or active caregivers. A further strength of the sample is the ethnic diversity of the family members. Approximately 50 percent of the respondents were persons of color and 50 percent were white. The distribution of parents was 37 percent. At the first interview with family members, about 17 percent of respondents reported that the consumer was a member of their household. Less than 10 percent were members of an organized family group.

The household member column shows that 52.3 percent of household members were female with an average age of 31; 54.7 percent were black; about 29 percent lived in a household with a 1988 income of less than $10,000 a year; and the households they lived in averaged 3.5 persons (excluding the consumers). The 958 household members held a variety of kin relationships to the consumer including: parent, child, spouse, sibling, stepmother, stepfather, cousin, niece, nephew, half-sister, half-brother, grandson, granddaughter, son-in-law, aunt, uncle, and ex-spouse.

As is shown in the household unit column, slightly more than half of the household units were associated with a female consumer. As has been reported before, the households were not affluent. (Family respondents reported household income, not personal income.) Almost one-third reported household income of less than $10,000 for the year 1988. Less than 3 percent reported income of more than $70,000. The average age of the household unit was 37.5 years and ranged from 7.4 to 80. The unit with an average age of 7.4 consisted of a consumer's 33-year-old sister and eight minor children ranging in age from 1 to 8 years, and the unit with an average age of 80 was a one-person household consisting of an 80-year-old grandmother. None of these characteristics significantly distinguished co-resident from non-co-resident household units.

Family type was stable, with only trivial changes over time. At all three points in time the most frequently reported family type was the parental household. About 37 percent of the household units included the consumer's natural or adoptive parents but no relatives of the marital family. Another 2.5 percent included parents and/or siblings as well as the consumer's spouse, children, and/or grandchildren. About one-fourth of the households were independent households of the consumer's siblings that did not include parents. Twelve percent were households that included spouses and/or children and grand-children. Fourteen percent were households of the consumer's sec-ondary kin such as aunts and grandparents. The remaining 11 percent were composed of friends, acquaintances, significant others, room-mates, foster parents, ex-spouses, and step- and in-law-*only* members.

Co-Residence and Family Type

Once again, co-residence is a main focus. If we look only at the 60 co-resident households, we find that the majority of co-resident con-sumers lived in *parental* households, which averaged more than 40 percent of all co-resident situations over the course of the study. Only 24 households or 9 percent were those whose members consisted only of parents; however, more than 40 percent of these were co-resident at one or more points in time.

Of the remaining 60 percent of co-resident situations, the *family of procreation* was next in importance, furnishing more than one-fourth of co-resident households. Surprisingly, *fictive kin* was the third most important housing resource, providing up to one-fifth of co-residence, with the *extended family* contributing another 8 percent. *Sibling* households ranked near the bottom, and *secondary kin* house-holds were least likely to be co-resident, with only one consumer living with a grandmother.

However, when we look at all households and within a particular family type, the analysis showed proportionately the most co-residence for the extended family, with more than one-third of these co-resident. Next is the marital family, with more than one-fourth of these households co-resident compared with the parental family, with one-fifth co-resident. Of course there are many more parental fami-lies represented, and thus more parental families who experience co-residence as noted above. We also observed the importance of fictive kin, which includes boyfriends, girlfriends, and friends.

The Involvement of Household Members

The perceived involvement of household members and units was the variable of major interest. The level of involvement averaged over the three points in time and reported for all household members is 1.6 or between *slightly* and *somewhat* involved. Average involvement scores for household units did not differ substantively from individual household member scores and also averaged between *slightly* and *somewhat* involved

Before reporting the involvement of vulnerable younger and older persons, we will describe these two groups. Almost one-third of the household members, or 306 persons, were children and adolescents under the age of 18, with an average age of 8.2 years, ranging from newborn to age 17. The sex of the children was almost evenly distributed, with 50.5 percent males and 49.5 percent females. As might be expected, these children include the sons and daughters of the consumer. However, the consumer's offspring made up less than 15 percent of the children. The most frequently reported young relatives were nieces and nephews who, of course, are the children of the consumer's adult brothers and sisters. Almost half of the minor children present in respondent households were in this category. Also included were younger brothers and sisters, grandchildren, cousins, step-relationships, and "friends." One-fourth of the children were co-resident with the consumer because the consumer also lived in the respondent's household.

The 121 older household members (defined as 62 or older) were for the most part the parents of the consumer. But households also included older spouses, grandmothers, grandfathers, one great-grandmother, aunts and uncles, and friends. Forty-seven percent were males and 53 percent were females.

Relationship significantly structured the perceived involvement of children and adolescents. Daughters and sons were most involved, scoring between *somewhat* and *very* involved, as did granddaughters and sisters. The children's sex also had an effect, with brothers scoring only *slightly involved*. Grandsons were less involved than granddaughters. Cousins and step-relationships all scored between *not involved* and *slightly* involved. Children reported as having no relationship to the consumer had the lowest perceived involvement scores.

Compared with adult household members, children are perceived as less involved. Children averaged a score of 1.5 on the involvement item compared with 1.7 for adults, a difference that is statistically but not substantively significant. On average, neither group appears to be perceived as strongly involved, with both groups' involvement scores falling between *slightly* and *somewhat* involved. However, there is no significant difference in involvement scores between adult and child household members when co-resident with the consumer. Both groups average between *somewhat* and *very* involved.

There is also no statistically significant difference between adult household members over 61 and those 61 or younger. Both groups of adults averaged between *slightly* and *somewhat* involved.

We also looked at the association between family type and involvement for the household *unit*. Involvement scores are significantly related to family type. When involvement scores are summed and averaged over the household unit, the extended family household units reported the highest level of involvement or close to *very involved*, followed by the parental family, the marital family, the sibling family, and fictive kin. The secondary kin household unit had the lowest average involvement scores, averaging near *slightly* involved.

Multivariate Analyses

We modeled both household member and household unit total involvement scores, averaged over the three points in time, as functions of the following consumer and household member (or unit) characteristics: age, sex, family role, total co-residence, income, total house size, case management history, and consumer symptoms, diagnosis, and marital status.

Age had no effect on the involvement scores of either household members or units. The sex of individual household members was marginally associated with greater involvement, with females tending to be more involved than males. However, the proportion of females living in a household unit had no significant effect. As expected, the relationships of parent, spouse, and child were associated with significantly higher involvement scores compared with siblings, secondary, and fictive kin for both household members and units. In addition, and as expected for both members and units, total co-residence predicted higher involvement. Low income predicted higher involvement for the household member but not the household unit, and the results are similar for house size.

The effect of consumer characteristics varied somewhat, based on the unit of analysis. For both members and units there was significantly more involvement when the consumer reported a history of continuous case management. In addition, the greater the average number and severity of symptoms reported by the consumer over three interviews, the less involved were both members and units. A diagnosis of schizophrenia was significantly associated with less involvement for members but not for units. When the consumer had never been married, household members tended to be more involved, and household units were significantly more involved.

DISCUSSION

Given the agreement in the literature that females are more often caregivers and more often linked to the emotional work within a household, we expected that the proportion of females in a household would have a positive effect on involvement scores. Yet at the household *unit* level of analysis, the members' sex had no effect. However, at the individual level of analysis, female household members reported feeling more involved than male household members, as expected.

A number of other findings merit summary. Controlling for sex, the primary relationships of parent, spouse, and child were associated with significantly higher involvement scores compared with siblings and secondary and fictive kin. Relationship to the person with mental illness structures involvement with him or her for both co-resident and non-co-resident household members. Low income was associated with more household member involvement, which may reflect the disposition for persons with limited financial resources to provide support and help instead of goods and money. However, the low household income effect did not extend to household size. Perhaps because the number of people living in the household is strongly associated with family type, household size does not have an independent effect on how involved household members are with the relative with mental illness.

In terms of the ages of the household members, an important finding is that vulnerable younger and older household members are no less involved with the relative with mental illness than are other, presumably less vulnerable, members of the household. Mental health professionals should consider the presence or absence of children and elderly members in co-resident households when planning for family support. The impact of mental illness on these household members remains unknown, but there is surely reason to give them special attention.

It is not coincidental that research has tended to focus on the family of origin. The parental household is an important housing resource for adults with mental illness, perhaps *the* most important resource, comprising 44 percent of co-resident households in this longitudinal study. However, the remaining 56 percent of the households under study embody many other configurations of kin. Although fewest in absolute numbers, the extended family type is associated with the greatest level of household unit involvement. This is followed by the family of procreation, which, when it exists, is also an important source of household involvement. Sibling and secondary kin family types are the least important family types in terms of co-residence with the relative with mental illness. In only one case did a secondary kin share housing with a consumer.

Perhaps the most important conclusion is that the family impact of mental illness potentially extends far beyond primary, or even secondary, caregivers. As we have shown, the family burden of mental illness is not limited to the family members who choose to provide care, supervision, or money. Even if they have no caregiving duties or financial responsibilities whatsoever, many household members are personally involved with the relative with mental illness, and their experiences—whether positive or negative—represent an important part of the total picture.

PART III

Family Experiences in Ohio: 1995–1997

Chapter 9

The Research Landscape Revisited

By the mid-1990s, major changes had taken place in Ohio's public mental health system, mirroring changes in many other states. Ohio was witnessing the rise of managed care, and with it, the promise of cost containment and increased efficiency (Hoge et al. 1994; Mechanic 1994, 1999). Family members were becoming more involved in system planning and as partners in treatment, the Ohio Alliance for the Mentally Ill had become an important player in the Ohio state legislature, and the National Alliance had become an important voice in the U.S. Congress in Washington, D.C., where mental health lobbyists advocated for parity with general health care insurance benefits (NAMI 1997).

Despite these changes in the mental health landscape, the issues facing family members of relatives with serious and persistent mental illnesses remained much the same, namely, whether and how to assist in activities of daily living, whether and how to exercise control over behavior problems, and whether and how to provide financial support. Without a cure for serious mental illnesses, family members in Ohio and elsewhere continued to worry about their ill relatives and about their own caregiving responsibilities.

In this chapter, we describe the sociopolitical context of the mid-1990s that confronted not only family members, but also service providers and consumers. Although the stakeholders were largely the same as those we met in the late 1980s, their concerns had evolved and there were new issues that needed to be addressed for new research to be timely and relevant. The challenge we faced as researchers was how to address the emergent issues in public mental health in a way that would be objective and that could inform all of the stakeholders. Since our research was both supported and sponsored by the Ohio Department of Mental Health (ODMH), we will refer to it as the ODMH family study.

BACKGROUND TO THE ODMH FAMILY STUDY

The ODMH family study was conducted by the University of Massachusetts at Amherst from 1995 to 1997 in response to the changes in mental health policy noted above. Beginning in 1995 under an expected waiver from the federal Health Care Financing Administration (HCFA), the state of Ohio planned the mandatory enrollment of Medicaid beneficiaries in a managed health care system (Ohio-Care). Under the Medicaid waiver, the Ohio Department of Mental Health would have received funds prospectively based on a capitated rate and, in collaboration with its system of county boards, would have been responsible for managing the *formal system* of mental health care of all Medicaid-eligible persons.

Based upon the expected implementation of OhioCare, we designed a study of the family impact of managed mental health care. Our research design called for three family member interviews, one prior to the implementation of OhioCare, and two following, in which we were interested in looking at the effects of system changes on the family burden and on family evaluations of mental health services. Although the main beneficiaries of managed care were intended to be primary consumers, family members who represent the *informal system* of care were also likely to be affected.

The state of Ohio received *federal* approval for a Medicaid waiver. However, OhioCare was not approved by the Ohio state legislature for the provision of mental health services. Even though approval was not received for the "carve-out" of Special Health Related Services, ODMH continued to work in the direction of managed care. Despite the loss of the legislation for the mental health carve-out part of OhioCare, most of the boards were still moving toward managed care in some fashion by restructuring their service systems and doing things such as instituting a single point of intake or beefing up crisis and emergency services. Some boards were still continuing to meet with one another in alliance groupings that were forming to become Managed Care Entities. In addition, ODMH would become the payer on some transfer services, and health maintenance organizations would provide some low-level, first-line mental health services (Dee Roth, personal communication).

The Ohio Department of Mental Health has long been a leader in recognizing the importance of the family members of persons with mental illness in the informal system of care—acknowledging their burdens and encouraging their involvement in system and treatment planning. Rather than give up on the research, we continued our study on the assumption that system changes were taking place about which family members had strong feelings, and that it was valuable to record those family sentiments. Thus, ODMH decided to continue the study of family experiences with mental illness, focusing on family member satisfaction with the public system of care and how family member evaluations changed as the system of care moved in the direction of managed care. The basic strategy was to generate a family sample linked to a longitudinal client study already being conducted by the ODMH.

RESEARCH DESIGN, SAMPLING, AND METHODS

The research design was a three-wave panel survey of family members linked to a second study, the Longitudinal Study of Mental Health Services and Consumer Outcomes in a Changing System (LCO) initiated by the Ohio Department of Mental Health in 1989 (Roth et al. 1994).

As described above, the ODMH family study was designed to evaluate the experiences of family members of persons with serious mental illness in the context of changes in the Ohio public system of care. Interviews were administered by trained interviewers from the Institute for Survey Research using a Computer Assisted Telephone Interview format. This format has several advantages, including reducing interviewer error, efficient data entry, and reduced costs.

The family member telephone interviews took place in 1995, 1996, and 1997. Data in the analyses were drawn from three sources: the LCO client interviews, the ODMH family interviews, and the state

Figure 9.1
Time Line of LCO Client and ODMH Family Member Data
Collections

1991	1992	1993	1995	1996	1997

LCO CLIENT INTERVIEWS

C_1 C_2 C_3 C_4

FAMILY MEMBER INTERVIEWS

F_1	F_2	F_3
N=147	N=126	N=113
Wave 1	Wave 2	Wave 3

Mental Health Information System (MHIS), which records client use of services. Figure 9.1 shows the timing of the family interviews in relation to the client interviews.

SAMPLING

The client sample is an extension of the LCO study initiated by the ODMH in 1989. To be included, clients had to meet the ODMH's 508 criteria for serious mental illness, and be receiving publicly funded mental health services. The sample was drawn from seven community mental health centers in four county board sites and stratified on patterns of service delivery, and, in two of the sites, further stratified by race. This original client sample consisted of 457 individuals, of whom 370 (81%) had been interviewed at three points in time as we planned the family study. The 370 individuals were 57 percent female, 21 percent African-American, and averaged 46 years of age; just less than half had received diagnoses of schizophrenia, 60 percent were high school graduates, and 13 percent were married throughout the initial three years of data collection (Roth et al. 1994).

ODMH continued the LCO longitudinal study, with a fourth interview with these same clients in the summer of 1995. At the end of this interview, the LCO interviewers explained that the family study would help the ODMH better understand the issues and problems that families have when a member has a serious mental illness and asked for longitudinal permission to contact family members by telephone. Employing a consent form designed especially for this purpose, the public sector clients in the LCO study nominated family members to be interviewed. If clients consented, they were asked to provide up to three names of family members, including addresses and telephone numbers, with the understanding that only *one* family member would actually be interviewed three times over a two-year period. LCO clients were informed that their family members would be paid a $10 honorarium per interview in appreciation of their time and effort.

Also as part of this process, clients were asked about primary kin they count on from time to time. Clients were asked in sequence if they could count on their mother, father, brother, sister, husband, wife, son, or daughter. In this way we gathered information about the clients' primary kinship networks *before* asking for their consent to interview family members.

Consent/refusal forms were received from all 323 clients who completed a fourth LCO interview. Most clients had family members, but four consumers were deemed ineligible for the family study because they literally had no relatives of any kind. Of the 323 LCO clients, 188 (58.2%) consented to have a family member interviewed.

Clients who refused gave a variety of reasons for not wanting their family members to participate. The reasons given for refusing had three general themes: Some clients refused to nominate relatives out of *concern* for their family members. Consumers believed a telephone interview would be too difficult for relatives who were in poor health or had trouble hearing. In a few cases, clients did not refuse but reported that their family members were without a telephone or, in even more serious cases, homeless. Other clients admitted to family *difficulties* arising from the mental illness and believed they could no longer count on family members to be supportive. In some circumstances, consumers believed that family members don't understand mental illness, and some reported that their relatives refused to accept that there is an illness. A few clients reported being angry with family members and in extreme cases being afraid of certain relatives. A few consumers reported little or *no contact* with family, in rare cases for more than a decade (Tessler et al. 1998).

The first interviews took place in 1995 (Wave 1) with 147 family members. A second wave of interviews took place in 1996 (Wave 2) when 126 family members were re-interviewed. A third wave was conducted in 1997 (Wave 3) when a total of 113 relatives (linked to

113 clients) were re-interviewed for the third and final time. It is the 113 family members (and their relatives) who completed all three interviews that form the basis for the analyses presented in this section of the book.

FAMILY MEMBER ATTRITION

An important issue in longitudinal research is attrition. As research subjects drop out of a study over time, it is important to understand the ways in which the characteristics of the final sample may differ from those of the original sample, before we describe the sample of 113 family members who completed all three interviews.

We succeeded in obtaining a first telephone interview in 1995 with 147 family members out of the 188 clients who gave permission. This is a 78.2 percent response rate. Interviews were conducted by a professional survey firm using a Computer Assisted Telephone Interview format. Most of the time when we could not obtain a family interview it was because we were unable to reach or find a family member— even after extensive help from the ODMH. When family members were reached by telephone in 1995, the cooperation rate was almost 90 percent.

A total of 126 family members were interviewed in 1996 out of the 147. Reasons for the attrition of the 20 family members between Wave 1 and Wave 2 included the death of the client (4), no valid telephone number (5), unable to locate (5), family member refused (4), and no reason given (2).

A total of 113 family members were interviewed in 1997 out of the 126. Reasons for non-interviews between Wave 2 and Wave 3 included the death of the client (n = 2), the death of the family member (n = 3), family member was deaf or incapacitated (n = 2), unable to find family member (n = 2), family member refused (n = 3), and never available (n = 1). Further information about family member attrition is available in the authors' final report to the ODMH (Gamache and Tessler 1998).

FM AND RMI CHARACTERISTICS

As is shown in Table 9.1, the 113 family members (FMs) averaged 53 years of age (range 22–88), had slightly more than 12 years of education, were 81 percent female, and were 76 percent white; only

Table 9.1
Characteristics of Family Members and Their Relatives with Mental Illness (N = 113)

Variable	Family Members	Relatives with Mental Illness
Race (% black)	24.0	21.2
Sex (% female)	81.0	53.1
Age (mean years)	52.8	48.1
Education (mean years)	12.2	11.0
Co-Residence (%)	33.6	-
Primary Caregiver (%)	75.0	-
Schizophrenia (%)	-	45.4

8 percent were currently members of NAMI, and 56 percent reported 1997 household income of $15,000 or less. Some 75 percent said they provided the most support for their relative with mental illness (RMI). Some 36 percent of the 113 family members were parents, 20 percent were adult children, 18 percent were spouses, 17 percent were siblings, 6 percent were other relatives, and 3 percent were fictive kin. Other relatives included two aunts, one cousin, one cousin-in-law, one sister-in-law, and one uncle. The three fictive kin identified themselves as a guardian, a caregiver, and a mental health professional (all three were female). Just over one-third of interviewed family members reported co-residence with their relative with mental illness during at least one of the interviews. Based on family member reports, we estimate that another 20 percent of the RMIs were living with family members who were not interviewed, thus indicating a high level of *total* FM residential involvement with the RMIs.

At the time of their third interview in 1997, a total of 98 percent of the FMs reported being in contact with their RMI during the past 30 days; the remaining 2 percent reported seeing, talking to, or having knowledge of their RMI during the past six months. Almost three-fourths reported that their relative has a case manager, primary therapist, or social worker that he or she saw on a regular basis.

Table 9.1 also shows the characteristics of the 113 *relatives with mental illness*. They averaged 48 years of age (ranging from 22 to 78) and 11 years of education, 53 percent were female, and 45 percent had received a diagnosis of schizophrenia. A total of 30.1 percent were living in southern Ohio/Appalachia along the Ohio River; 27.4 percent in northwest Ohio; 27.4 percent in Montgomery County, mainly in the city of Dayton; and 15 percent in the Trumbull County site in northeast Ohio (the Youngstown/Warren area).

To provide further information about the consumers of mental health services, records were obtained by the ODMH about the actual usage of 21 certified mental health services by the relatives with mental illness. The 113 LCO clients received 14 of the 21 possible services. These included crisis intervention, diagnostic assessment, medication/somatic, individual counseling/therapy, group counseling/therapy, prehospitalization/screening, employment service, vocational service, partial hospitalization, residential treatment comprehensive, residential treatment facility, residential support, community residence, and case management (group or individual). None of the 113 clients associated with an interviewed family member received the following services: adult education, adjunctive therapy, occupational therapy, school psychology, inpatient services, forensic services, or the category called "other certified mental health services."

An index constructed from the 14 certified mental health services that the 113 clients did receive indicates that 24 percent received no certified mental health services of any kind. An additional 29 percent of clients received one service, 22 percent received two services, and 16 percent received three services. The remaining 9 percent received from four to eight services. The most commonly reported service was case management (group or individual); 77 percent of the 113 clients received this service. This was followed by "medication/somatic"; about 69 percent received this service.

CURRENT ISSUES

Family Involvement in the System of Care

Family members have long sought the right to be consulted about treatment planning, and in recent years professional barriers to family involvement have indeed been on the wane. But are there, and should there be, consumer barriers to family involvement? What do RMIs and FMs actually want and expect from one another in terms of their respective involvements in the public system of care? To explore these issues, we collected basic information about the preferences of family members as to their involvement in their relative's treatment and the preferences of their relatives as perceived by the interviewed FMs. Drawing on official data on the use of certified mental health services, we also examine how family and professional involvement interact with each other. Are the formal and informal systems of care mutually enhancing, or is one a substitute for the other? Chapter 10 presents the research findings.

Evaluating Services Under Managed Care

When OhioCare was not implemented, the opportunity to systematically evaluate managed care was lost. But it was still possible to evaluate many of the services and system characteristics that would be integral to any managed care policy. With this goal in mind, we developed a new set of measures intended for use with family members to summarize their evaluations of mental health professionals, services, and systems. Our previous research indicated moderate to high levels of family member satisfaction with professionals, but it has been difficult in attitudinal research to distinguish personal feelings toward providers from satisfaction with the services and systems (Tessler, Gamache, and Fisher 1991). We hoped these new measures would be more appropriate to eliciting family evaluations that distinguished professionals from services and systems. The results are reported in Chapter 11.

Insurance Parity

In the third wave of family interviews in 1997, we included a special module designed to use family members as informants about the history of their relatives' mental health insurance coverage. We were particularly interested in learning whether relatives with mental illness had previously been covered by private plans before becoming a part of the public system of care. Without "parity" in insurance coverage, of the sort that is routinely available outside of mental health, we expected to find that the vast majority of the relatives with serious and persistent mental illness would have had no viable alternative to the public system of care. We also asked family members how important the issue of parity was to them. The findings from the insurance module will be discussed in Chapter 12.

In the remainder of this book, we revisit the research landscape in

Ohio, focusing on the emergent issues that were being discussed in mental health policy circles nationwide. By the mid-1990s, the research landscape in Ohio had changed to include new issues of concern to family members and family advocates that had not been salient even five years before. Family researchers who had once limited their focus to informal caregiving and burden now had to enlarge their foci to include such issues as the family impact of managed mental health care, strategies for achieving parity between psychiatric and general health insurance coverage, and ways to institutionalize family involvement in the public system of care.

Chapter 10

How Much Involvement Do Family Members Want?

In an era of community care for consumers of mental health services, building health systems should involve family members. Thus, it is to be expected that another significant element of change in Ohio (as elsewhere) is the encouragement of family participation at the individual, county, and state levels with the goal of enhancing cooperation and communication between clients, family members, and professionals.

In response to the empowerment of both family members and consumers, who have each organized their own advocacy groups, state mental health authorities nationwide have implemented plans to include family and consumer representation on state planning committees, advisory boards, and as speakers and panelists at conferences. But typically, public systems of care involve only those family members and consumers who choose to come forward, often as representatives of organized groups. The problem is that these individuals may not be representative of all family members or consumers.

Moreover, some family members may want to be involved, whereas their relatives with mental illness may prefer that they not be. Some consumers may want a lot of family involvement, whereas others may want as little as possible. Some consumers might feel strongly that family members should not be involved at all in building a system of care. Other consumers might feel positively about a family member being involved in system design issues but not in his or her treatment.

In contrast to some other types of caregiving (e.g., when a relative has a stroke), the caregiving role is potentially more conflicted, and how best to involve family members in systems building and treatment planning cannot be determined without also considering consumers' wishes. The parties involved may well have different opinions of what constitutes a responsive system of care, and about the role that family members should play in the consumer's treatment. Furthermore, family desires may vary as a function of caregiving rendered, whereas consumer desires may vary as a result of caregiving received.

The idea that empowering both consumers and family caregivers will lead to a better system of care, as well as more stakeholder satisfaction, certainly has merit, but as yet little empirical evidence is available to support it. In addition, the respective roles and potential conflicts between the two stakeholders regarding their preferences had not been systematically examined. Thus, a primary objective of our research was to collect basic information about both the preferences of family members as to their involvement in treatment, and their beliefs about the preferences of their relatives with mental illness for family involvement. How much involvement do family members want in their relative's treatment? How much do consumers of mental health services want family members involved, directly or indirectly, in their treatment? Can the system do both at the same time, that is, satisfy both consumer and family member preferences for involvement?

In the next sections, we examine several aspects of the relationship between family members (FMs) and their relatives with mental illness (RMIs). Using self-reports of family members, we describe how deeply involved FMs perceive themselves to be with their RMIs, whether or not FMs consider themselves to be primary caregivers for their RMIs, and how much involvement FMs want in the RMIs' treatment plan. We also examine the other side of family involvement, that is, the involvement of the RMI with his or her family, as indicated by reciprocal contributions that RMIs may be making to their FMs. Finally, we attempt to come full circle with our earlier research, presented in Part II of this book, by revisiting the issue of family burden.

Table 10.1
Family Member Involvement with Relative with Mental Illness
(N = 113)

Variable	1995	1996	1997	Total
How deeply FM is involved with RMI (mean)	3.72	3.6	3.59	3.64
FM provides most support to RMI (%)	86.7	78.2	75.0	97.3
FM wants to be involved in RMI's treatment (%)	76.1	69.4	73.5	93.7
RMI wants FM to be involved in treatment (%)	66.4	59.3	71.0	65.5
RMI contributions to FM (mean)	1.58	1.43	1.42	1.49

DEPTH OF FM INVOLVEMENT WITH RMI

We inquired about how *deeply involved* FMs perceived themselves to be with their RMIs. Response categories were very (= 4), somewhat (= 3), slightly (= 2), and not (= 1) involved. As is shown in Table 10.1, the average *total* involvement score over the course of the study was 3.64 (or close to "very involved"). This was not unexpected, since RMIs were asked to nominate family members that they counted on to help them out from time to time. Moreover, those FMs who were motivated to participate in all three interviews would be likely to define themselves as very, or at least somewhat, involved with their RMI.

In 1995, the average self-reported involvement score was 3.72. By 1996, the average involvement score had decreased to 3.59, which represented a statistically significant decline ($t = 2.2$, p =.03). Scores were nearly identical in 1996 and 1997 (3.50 versus. 3.59). However, the drop in self-reported involvement between 1995 and 1997 was also statistically significant (one-tailed test, $t = 1.74$, p =.04).

PRIMARY CAREGIVERS

FMs were also asked whether or not they considered themselves to be primary caregivers (the family members "who provide the most support") for their RMIs, coded "yes" (=1) or "no" (=0). As is also shown in the *Total* column in Table 10.1, some 97 percent of family members defined themselves in this way at least once during the course of the study. This was also not unexpected for the reasons cited above.

On the other hand, the proportion of family members who considered themselves as primary caregivers in any given year did vary over the course of the study, from a high of 87 percent to a low of 75 percent. Such variation is consistent with the idea that relations between FMs and RMIs are accordionlike, going in and out of closeness (Stoneall 1983).

DESIRED INVOLVEMENT IN TREATMENT

We also empirically addressed the question of how much involvement family members wanted to have in their relatives' treatment plans during the six months prior to each of the three interviews. In 1995, some 76 percent of family members said they wanted "some" or "a lot" of involvement in their relatives' treatment plan (rather than "very little" or "none at all"). The proportion of family members wanting "some" or "a lot" of involvement decreased from 76.1 percent in 1995 to 69.4 percent in 1996. But the proportion did not significantly change between 1996 and 1997, when some 73.5 percent wanted "some" or "a lot" of involvement. Only seven FMs (6%) wanted "less" than "some" or "a lot" of involvement over the entire course of the study.

We also asked family members, at each interview, how much involvement they thought their *relatives wanted* them to have in their treatment plans during the same time periods. In 1995, some 66.4 percent of family members reported that their relatives wanted them to have "some" or "a lot" of involvement in the treatment plan. This proportion had significantly decreased by 1996 to 59.3 percent. It may be that after being asked this question in 1995, some family members discussed the issue with their relative and discovered they had overestimated the amount of involvement that he or she wanted. However, by 1997, the proportion of FMs reporting that their RMIs wanted them to have "some" or "a lot" of involvement in their treatment plans had increased to 70.8 percent.

IS FAMILY INVOLVEMENT A TWO-WAY STREET?

Although mental illness may constrain RMI autonomy and encourage dependency, it does not necessarily rule out exchanges between RMIs and their families (Horwitz, Reinhards, and Howell-White 1996). Research language tends to ignore the fact that a consumer of mental health services is a family member, too, and as such may give help with household chores, offer a sympathetic ear, or, quite importantly, provide companionship. To the extent that such client contributions do occur, they may offset some of the other burdens that are present. On the other hand, when a relative fails to fulfill family role obligations, the resulting strain may damage relationships.

Our measure of client contributions is derived from the National Survey of Families and Households and is taken from the National Surveys of Families and Households (Sweet, Bumpass, and Call 1988). The rationale is to describe what, if anything, the RMI has done recently to benefit the FM.

The measure includes five items describing what the RMI may have done for the family member during the past 30 days. Interviewers followed the statement, "Here is a list of things that family members sometimes do for one another" with the question:

Please tell me how often *during the past 30 days (your relative)* has done the following for you: helped you with meal preparation, shopping or other household chores (helped you out financially, offered advice, given you news about family members or mutual friends, and given you companionship)? Response categories were: not at all = 0, less than once a week = 1, once or twice a week = 2, 3 to 6 times a week = 3, every day = 4.

Examination of the relevant data in Table 10.1 reveals that on average, FMs reported receiving contributions from the RMI between "less than once a week" and "once or twice a week" during all three measurement periods (1995 = 1.58; 1996 = 1.43; 1997 = 1.42). Two-tailed t-tests indicate that the differences between 1995 and 1996 (t = 2.1, p = .04) and 1995 and 1997 (t = 2.4, p = .02) were significant. However, the difference between 1996 and 1997 was not significant.

In summary, a moderate amount of patient contributions were reported, even though the majority of RMIs were not living with the interviewed FMs. Thus, in most cases family involvement was not a one-way proposition, although it was not fully reciprocal, either (also see Chapter 7).

FAMILY ROLE AND CO-RESIDENCE

Examination of Table 10.2 shows that there were significant differences by family role with respect to "how deeply involved" FMs

Table 10.2
Involvement by Family Role and Living Arrangements (N = 113)

Variable	n^1	How deeply FM is Involved with RMI	FM is Primary Community Support	FM Wants Involvement in RMI Treatment	RMI Wants FM Involvement in Treatment	RMI Helps FM
Family Role		Mean[*]	% (of 3)[#]	% (of 3)	% (of 3)[*]	Mean[****]
Parent	41	3.67	80.0	70.1	58.5	1.22
Spouse	20	3.91	94.7	85.0	83.3	3.04
Siblings	19	3.61	85.2	70.2	71.9	1.19
Adult Children	23	3.48	74.2	67.7	52.2	1.08
Other Kin	7	3.29	61.9	71.4	76.2	.85
Fictive Kin	3	3.67	66.7	100.0	77.8	1.40
Living Arrangements		Mean[***]	% of 3[***]	% of 3[#]	% (of 3)[**]	Mean[****]
Co-Resident	45	3.82	92.0	66.7	57.6	2.23
Not Co-Resident	66	3.51	72.5	82.2	76.6	.95

Notes: [1]n's may vary due to missing data; [****]p <.0001; [***]p <.0001; [**]p <.01; [*]p <.05; [#]p <.10; one-tailed *t*-tests.

perceived themselves to be with their RMIs over the course of the study. Reflecting the hierarchy of family obligations to adult members, spouses' self-reports of involvement (3.91) were the highest of any family role. Parents and fictive kin (3.67) scored the next highest in terms of involvement.

As expected, co-resident family members reported significantly higher involvement (3.82) with their RMIs than did FMs who did not live with relatives (3.51). Even so, it is impressive that the non-co-resident family members felt as much involvement as they reported.

Table 10.2 also shows the cross-tabulation of *Total Prime* (the proportion of interviews, out of three, that the FM claimed to be the RMI's primary caregiver by family role (parent, spouse, etc.). There was a marginally significant trend (p = .06) for some family roles to be more associated with primary caregiving than other family roles. On average, spouses (.95) were most likely to see themselves as primary caregivers, followed by siblings (.85), parents (.80), adult children (.74), fictive kin (.66), and other relatives (.62). In interpreting these differences, it is important to remember that these family members participated in the study because they were involved with the RMIs.

As expected, co-resident FMs were significantly more likely to view themselves as primary caregivers (92%) than were non-co-resident family members (72.5%). But once again, the proportion of non-co-resident family members in the study who viewed themselves as primary supports is quite impressive.

There was no significant relationship between family role and FM wishes for "some" or "a lot" of involvement in the RMI's treatment plan. However, the desire for involvement in treatment plans depended on whether the RMI was living with the FM. Surprisingly non-co-resident FMs were significantly more likely to say they wanted a high level of involvement in treatment planning (82.2%) than were co-resident FMs (66.7%). Perhaps co-resident family members had seen enough of treatment plans and wished more for distance from this aspect of their relationship to the RMIs.

FMs' perceptions of their RMIs' desires to have them involved in treatment did vary significantly by family role. Over the course of the study, spouses (83.3%), fictive kin (77.8%), and other kin (76.2%) were most likely to report that their RMI desired at least "some," if not "a lot," of involvement. Siblings (71.9%) and parents (58.5%) were somewhat less likely to believe that their RMI wanted them to be strongly involved in their treatment, and adult children were least likely to hold this belief (52.2%).

Again, non-co-resident FMs were significantly more likely (76.6%) to report that their RMIs wanted a higher level of involvement than were co-resident FMs (57.6%). These unexpected differences merit further research, since they suggest different barriers to involvement among family members under different conditions of co-residence.

The contributions of RMIs also varied significantly by family role. Spouses (3.04) reported, by far, receiving the most contributions. Fictive kin were next (1.4), followed by parents (1.22), siblings (1.19), and adult children (1.08). Other relatives reported the fewest contributions (.85).

Also, and as expected, co-resident family members reported significantly more contributions (2.33) than did non-co-resident family members (.95).

FAMILY BURDEN DURING 1995–1997

Although not all of the measures were the same, it appeared that we actually detected *more* family burden in 1995–1997 than in our prior research in Ohio during 1989–1992. However, average levels of both objective and subjective burden remained in the mild to moderate range.

For example, family members reported assisting the RMI with tasks of daily living on an average of less than once a week, in part because 11 FMs (9.7%) provided no assistance with the activities of daily living during the period 1995–1997. Even when they did provide Care, FMs only rarely said they "minded" doing so. Although reports of Control were even less frequent, family members (like those in 1989–1992) "minded more" this form of assistance.

To measure Financial Burden, we used the same questions as we had in 1989–1992 (see Chapter 5). Family members were asked, "During the past 30 days, have you *personally* paid for, or given the client money for any of the following for which he or she has not paid you back?" As before, the list included such expenses as transportation, clothing, pocket money, food, rent, medication, mental health treatment, other medical expenses, cigarettes, and personal items. The numbers (and proportions) of family members (out of 113) giving money in at least one area were 47 FMs (42%) in 1995, 42 (37%) in 1996, and 43 (38%) in 1997. Over the three interviews, 60 percent of family members reported giving money to their RMIs in at least one area. When asked about the subjective burden of financial support, family members rarely said that giving money to the RMI had caused them hardship, even though these family members (like those surveyed before) were mainly a low income group. Of the various family roles, parents reported the most Financial contributions as well as the greatest hardship.

As expected, the burden of Care was higher when the family member was living with the relative with mental illness. Those who lived with their RMI provided more of this help and tended to mind helping more than those who were not living with their relatives. In contrast, neither Control nor Financial Burden was significantly associated with co-resident living arrangements.

Table 10.3
Changes in Objective Burden between 1995 and 1997 (N = 113)

	Means			T-Test Results		
Burden	1995	1996	1997	95 > 96	96 >97	95 > 97
FINANCIAL (% of 8 areas)	.127	.103	.099	p < .10	NS	p < .05
CARE (% of 8 areas)	.347	.288	.253	p < .01	p < .05	p < .001
CONTROL (% of 7 areas)	.110	.087	.104	p < .10	NS	NS

Note: NS = Not significant

The frequency of Care was positively and significantly correlated with both the number of services (r = .24, p <.05) and the variety of certified mental health services received (r = .191, p <.05), according to management information records for 1996. RMIs who received *no* formal services from the Department of Mental Health also received less Care from family members compared with those who received formal services. Similarly, Financial expenditures by family members also increased as a function of the number (r = .23, p <.05) and the variety of certified mental health services received (r = .289, p <.01). However, the frequency of Control was not significantly associated with RMI involvement in the professional system of care.

Did family burden change between 1995 and 1997 as the public system in Ohio was making the transition into managed care? This question was evaluated by comparing the proportion of areas in which family burden was experienced in each year. The results are shown in Table 10.3.

With respect to objective burden, only Care decreased steadily from the first to the second interview, and then from the second to the third. Financial Burden also declined during these same periods, but the decrease was statistically significant only between 1995 and 1997. Control burden was the one exception to the pattern of declining objective burdens. It decreased slightly between 1995 and 1996, but then rose between 1996 and 1997, although the increase was not statistically significant.

None of the subjective burden measures showed a significant decline between 1995 and 1996. However, by 1997, subjective Financial Hardship, subjective Care and subjective Control all showed evidence of decline. An index of Worry, which summarizes how much the family member worries about the relative's safety, treatment, social life, physical health, living arrangements, how the client would manage financially without the family member, and the client's future prospects, showed no significant change over the course of the study. As measured, worry is assumed to be both a form of subjective burden and an expression of attachment (data not shown).

DISCUSSION

Although the data reported in this chapter derive mainly from the reports of family members, it will be critical in future research to include the perspective of the consumers of mental health services, as well as the perspective of providers. Consumers, professionals, and family members are, or should be, part of a "health care triad" (Haug 1994). All three parties form a triangle that is important to the success of long-term care in the community. To ignore the perspective of any one of the parties is to jeopardize the entire caregiving enterprise.

The positive associations between Care and Financial Burden and receiving certified mental health services run counter to the expectations of some critics of managed care who predicted that *fewer* formal services would be associated with *more* informal caregiving by family members motivated more by obligation than desire. Rather than the predicted negative associations, we find positive associations between formal and informal caregiving suggestive of a cooperative rather than a competitive relationship between professionals and families.

This finding adds to accumulating evidence in public mental health that relations between family members and mental health professionals are improving and that the two parties are more often working together in the interests of the relative with mental illness. We have also seen from the data presented in this chapter that professionals are recognizing the family's role in treatment and inviting them into treatment planning more than ever before. In general, the direction of change is positive. This change may also create a new dilemma for some family members because, as we have seen, not everyone wants to be part of the treatment team—even informally. Family members also recognize that their own desired involvement may sometimes be at odds with their RMI's wishes.

As we saw in Chapter 8, a family member need not be providing

Care, Control, or Financial support to be emotionally involved with a relative with mental illness, particularly if the RMI is also a household member. Like most families, those with a member with mental illness experience a variety of emotions toward one another, ranging from warmth and acceptance to anger and rejection. When the family member feels that the relative with mental illness is contributing to the family, instrumentally or expressively, the family dynamics tend to change in the most positive of ways. When, on the other hand, the family member feels that the relative with mental illness is not doing his or her share, resentment is more likely to ensue. Mental health professionals need to help consumers of mental health services who are living in the community recognize their own responsibility to contribute to their families and to reciprocate the help and attention received from family members within the limits of their capabilities.

The evolution of managed care in Ohio does *not* appear to have markedly increased family burden. To the contrary, when change in the level of family member burden did occur between 1995 and 1997, it was most likely to be in the direction of lower burden. Whether this indicates the growing independence of consumers of mental health services, or a subtle disengagement on the part of aging family members, cannot be discerned from these data. But the finding that at least in Ohio, managed care is not substituting family involvement for professional involvement should be reassuring to all stakeholders.

Chapter 11

How Did Family Members Evaluate Professionals, Services, and Systems?

The purpose of this chapter is to introduce new measures for evaluating family experiences with mental health and allied professionals, services, and systems of care. We present a narrative history of the new measures, including how they were derived, how they were pilot tested, and how well they perform psychometrically. We also illustrate how both individual items and a summary index can be used over time as a barometer of family reactions to changes in the organization and financing of mental health care. A final section tests some hypotheses about factors affecting family satisfaction.

BACKGROUND AND SIGNIFICANCE

Most mental health policy makers now take as a basic tenet that a system of care will be more effective when family caregivers play an active role in its design, implementation, and evaluation. They are joined by academic researchers who also believe that building comprehensive mental health systems and monitoring quality of care should involve family members (Fisher, Benson, and Tessler 1990; Biegel, Song, and Milligan 1995).

Such positive rhetoric notwithstanding, family input in public mental health is more the exception than the rule, and past studies of family attitudes toward mental health services and professionals have, for the most part, been negative. Some empirical evidence indicates "near-universal dissatisfaction" with services (Grella and Grusky 1989, 831). More recently, a study in Vermont using focus groups to explore family attitudes reported that "[f]amily members saw themselves as disregarded by the mental health system and often blamed for their relatives' mental illness" (Pulice, McCormick, and Dewees 1995). The authors of a study of 250 family members in New York State reported how the relatives of consumers viewed mental health professionals during the 1980s:

Family members have complained that they have lacked information about the patient's illness, that they have received inadequate advice on management issues, and the availability of services during times of crisis has been poor. They have reported coming away from interactions with professionals feeling guilty, frustrated, and helpless. They place mental health workers at the bottom of their list of useful supports. (Bernheim and Switalski 1988)

On the other hand, recent studies indicate some improvement in relationships between family members and professionals. A majority of family members in the evaluation of the Robert Wood Johnson program, discussed in Part II, felt that professionals were interested in what the family members could tell them. Most also agreed that professionals assured them they were not to blame and showed that they understood the problems faced by the family. However, the results also revealed that a majority believed that professionals did not give detailed information or include family members in treatment planning (Tessler, Gamache, and Fisher 1991). More recently another group of researchers reported that black caregivers in Cleveland were satisfied overall, whereas white caregivers were more likely to complain (Biegel, Song, and Milligan 1995).

A new generation of measures is needed to make family input truly useful to mental health service administrators. Existing measures of family satisfaction with professionals focus only indirectly on family evaluations of client services and systems of care. If family members are to have a "say" about the quality of services and how they are (or are not) organized into a coherent system, then measures are needed that go beyond family satisfaction with professionals. Such scales would need both to inform how, and in what ways, family members (FM) find the mental health system responsive or unresponsive to both their own needs as well as the needs of their relatives with mental illness (RMI). The central issues that new measures need to address are how family members evaluate their own involvement as partners in treatment, how they evaluate the quality of services provided directly to their relatives with mental illness, and how they evaluate the public mental health system more generally.

NARRATIVE HISTORY OF THE FAMILY MEMBER EVALUATION MEASURES

The family study was a logical extension of how the ODMH has historically perceived its mission to support family member evaluations of the public system of care. Thus, the items were developed in collaboration with ODMH, where input was sought from policy analysts, program managers, and a family and consumer advocate.

The authors worked closely with the ODMH in constructing specific items around goals that were important to administrators as well as to family members and consumers. The following goals were used as a basis for generating items: that client services be readily accessible; that different components of the formal system of care be well integrated; that crisis response be timely and convenient; that family members have the opportunity to be involved in treatment plans; that clients have program options from which to choose; and that in general the system of care be responsive to what clients and family members need and want.

A total of 25 questions were developed to indicate whether and to what extent family members believe that these goals were being met in the past six months. Response categories were modeled after those used in a study of family satisfaction with services in a northwestern state conducted by Grella and Grusky (1989). These are (1) none (not) at all, (2) very little, (3) don't know/ambivalent, (4) some, but not as much as you wanted, or (5) all that you wanted or needed.

The basic strategy was to make the response category labeled "all that you wanted or needed" indicate the highest level of satisfaction. The response categories were chosen to quantify level of satisfaction while taking account of variation in client needs and family member preferences for specific services and desires for involvement. For example, in response to the question, "How much information did you receive from mental health service providers about (*NAME*)'s illness?," a family member who received no information in the past six months and was dissatisfied with the lack of information was coded "none at all." By contrast, a family member who received no information from service providers in the past six months because none was sought or desired was coded "all that you wanted or needed." When an item was not applicable, such as when no services were needed or no crisis occurred, "all that you wanted or needed" was also an appropriate response. Response code 3, which was not read, was used only used if the respondent could not make up his or her mind or didn't know how to answer the question.

INDIVIDUAL ITEMS

Table 11.1 reports the scores for individual items for each year, as well as three-year-average scores for each item. The 25 items are rank-listed by the three-year averages, from most to least satisfaction. Recall that response categories are: none (not) at all = 1, very little = 2, don't know/ambivalent = 3, some, but not as much as you wanted = 4, and all that you wanted or needed = 5. Once again, FM = Family Member; RMI = Relative with Mental Illness.

The summary scores for 1995–1997 hover just below, or on the low end, of response code 3—some, but not as much as you wanted. Where changes did occur, the typical pattern was for the most satisfaction to be reported in 1995, and significantly less in 1996 and 1997 after the Ohio state legislature rejected the Medicaid "carve out" of mental health managed care.

CHANGE OVER TIME

The items detecting statistically significant change between 1995 and 1997 are shown in Table 11.2. The items have been ranked by amount of change, but recall that each of these items showed significant change. Also shown (in the bottom row) is the change in the summated 25-item index.

As shown, satisfaction ratings in response to these 12 items decreased significantly between 1995 and 1997. Among the areas of greatest negative change was family member perception of how available help was in a crisis at night or on the weekend, how much opportunity there was to complain to an agency, how much opportunity there was for the RMI to choose between service options, whether enough culturally specific services were offered to the RMI, how much help RMIs received from professionals in finding services out-

Table 11.1
Ranking of Evaluation Items

Item	1995	1996	1997	3-Year Avg.
How convenient were mental health services?	4.18	4.05	3.90	4.04
How available were general health services?	4.00	3.86	3.66	3.84
How much was FM satisfied with RMI's services?	3.99	3.84	3.62	3.82
How many needed mental health services were available?	3.81	3.46	3.63	3.63
How available were dental services?	3.74	3.47	3.37	3.53
How much flexibility was there in RMI's treatment plan?	3.64	3.40	3.53	3.52
How much was FM satisfied with role in treatment?	3.57	3.51	3.31	3.46
How much say did RMI have in services?	3.73	3.20	3.44	3.46
How much opportunity was there for RMI to choose service options?	3.70	2.98	2.91	3.20
How much did professionals help RMI to find other services?	3.35	2.61	2.88	2.94
How much did the system respond to wishes of FMs?	3.10	2.85	2.76	2.90
How much opportunity was there for FM to complain to an agency?	3.53	2.34	2.57	2.81
How much did professionals recognize burden of FMs?	2.88	2.85	2.66	2.80
How much help was available at night/weekend if there were a crisis?	3.53	2.26	2.44	2.74
How much opportunity was there for RMI to choose a case manager?	2.71	2.58	2.53	2.60
How much did professionals respond to FM's concerns?	2.73	2.55	2.48	2.59
How much say did FM have about services?	2.79	2.35	2.35	2.50
How many culturally specific services were there for RMI?	2.78	2.21	2.19	2.40
How much did FM have contact with professionals?	2.36	2.19	2.43	2.33
How much did professionals take account of FM's opinion?	2.42	2.27	2.27	2.32
How much information was given about WHOM to call if there were a crisis?	2.25	2.24	2.32	2.27
How much was FM encouraged to take an active role?	2.38	2.23	2.16	2.26
How much did professionals involve FM in treatment?	2.29	2.05	2.18	2.17
How much information was given about WHAT to do if there were a crisis?	2.27	1.91	2.16	2.11
How much information did FM receive about the illness?	2.11	2.04	2.04	2.06
Summary Scale	3.11	2.77	2.79	2.89

Table 11.2
Decreases in Evaluations between 1995 and 1997 (N = 113)

During the past 6 months how ...	1995	1997	Change
available was help in a crisis at night or on a weekend?	3.53	2.44	-1.1****
much opportunity was there for you to complain to an agency?	3.53	2.57	-.96****
much choice was there for RMI in service options?	3.70	2.91	-.79****
many culturally specific services were offered to RMI?	2.78	2.19	-.58***
much did professionals help to find other services, e.g. housing?	3.35	2.88	-.47**
much say did you have in RMI's services?	2.79	2.35	-.43**
available were dental services?	3.74	3.37	-.372*
much satisfaction with the services did your relative receive?	3.99	3.62	-.372**
much was the mental health system responding to wishes of FMs?	3.10	2.76	-.3363*
available were general health services?	4.0	3.66	-.3362*
much say did RMI have in services?	3.72	3.44	-.28*
convenient were mental health services?	4.18	3.90	-.27*
Family Member Evaluations Scale (all 25 items)	3.11	2.79	-.32***

Notes: ****p <.000; ***p <.001; **p <.01; *p <.05; one-tailed *t*-tests.

side the specialty mental health sector, such as housing, and how much influence the FM had in the RMI's services. Other areas in which FM satisfaction decreased, although more modestly than in the areas noted above, were FM evaluations of the availability of dental services; overall satisfaction with the services the RMI received; how much FMs felt that the mental health system was responding to their wishes; FM assessments of the availability of general health services; the amount of "say" that the RMI had in his or her service plan; and how convenient it was for the RMI to make use of mental health services.

It would appear from these data that the Ohio public mental health system was in transition between 1995 and 1997 following the legislative turndown of the mental health carve-out of OhioCare. It is tempting to go beyond the data to argue that systemic change resulting in uncertainty for family members is what accounts for the decline in satisfaction. But without a comparison group, such an inference can be made only in the most tentative of ways.

PSYCHOMETRICS AND SCALE CONSTRUCTION

As already noted, the 25 items were originally chosen to measure the six important dimensions of evaluations by family members. To sort among the 25 items, we first attempted to construct subscales based on the *a priori* categories of accessibility, involvement of family member in treatment plan, integration of service delivery systems, crisis response, client choice among options, and adequacy of the system of care for relatives with mental illness. However, factor analyses of the three-year average ratings showed that neither the number of factors nor the item loadings corresponded to the *a priori* framework.

Therefore we decided to use an *a posteriori* framework based on a two-factor varimax solution, which appears to fit the data best. The two factor solution incorporates 14 items (rather than 25). The two factors distinguish between FM evaluations of professionals and of mental health services.

Evaluating Professionals

The items that load on the factor "evaluating professionals" include the following eight items: (1) How much information did you receive from mental health service providers about your relative's illness? (2) How much information did you receive from mental health professionals about what to do if there were to be a crisis involving your relative? (3) How much information did you receive from mental health professionals about whom to call if there were to be a crisis involving your relative? (4) How much were you encouraged by mental health professionals to take an active role in your relative's treatment? (5) How much did mental health professionals respond to your concerns about your relative? (6) How much did mental health professionals take into account your ideas and opinions? (7) How much did mental health professionals involve you in your relative's treatment? and (8) How much contact did you have with any mental health professional on any matter pertaining to your relative's care?

Evaluating Mental Health Services

The items that load on the factor "evaluating mental health services" include the following six items: (1) How many mental health services were available for your relative that you thought were needed? (2) How much opportunity did your relative have to choose between different service options? (3) How convenient was it for your relative to use mental health services? (4) How much say did your relative have in the services that (he or she) received? (5) If your relative's needs had changed, how much flexibility would there have been in the treatment plan? and (6) How much satisfaction did you feel about the services your relative received?

A note of caution is appropriate as we conclude the discussion of the factor analysis. Decisions about which items to drop were made solely on psychometric grounds. For example, if an item did not discriminate well between the two factors, it was dropped. Ironically, many of the items that were dropped were among those previously reported to be most sensitive to changes over time. In addition, every item, regardless of its psychometric properties, is of potential relevance to a public mental health system. Thus, there may be good reasons to resist the temptation to prune the complete list of 25 items to achieve a purer factor structure.

Modeling Family Member Satisfaction

In this final section, we attempt to predict scores on the summary index based upon the full array of 25 items. In selecting independent variables from which to predict family satisfaction with professionals, services, and systems, we considered the following in our model: (1) how well FMs believe that their relatives are doing; (2) how burdened the FMs are; and (3) the actual mix and intensity of services used by their relatives. We reasoned that family satisfaction would be higher if FMs believed that their RMI was doing well, if FMs were not highly burdened, and if the RMI was making appropriate use of the formal system of care, as indicated by utilization record data.

Since at the time of the analysis the most recent utilization data that was available was for Ohio Fiscal Year 1996 (FY'96), we decided to base the analysis on the 1996 family interviews. The following theoretical variables were included in the explanatory model:

Client Functioning. We had originally hoped to use measures of client functioning based on the LCO client interviews. But since client interviews did not occur in 1996, the year for which we had utilization data (see Chapter 9, Figure 9.1), we were forced to derive a measure of client functioning from the family interviews. This proxy measure was based on changes in family member worries about the RMI between 1995 and 1996.

The construction of family member worry summarized how much the family members worried about their relatives' safety, treatment, social life, physical health, living arrangements, and financial and other future prospects. Where FMs worried less in 1996 than in 1995, they were coded 1; where FMs worried the same or more in 1996 compared with 1995, they were coded 0. About 54 percent worried less, and 46 percent expressed either the same amount of worry or they worried more.

Client Use of Services. Two variables were derived from the FY'96 record data: a measure of intensity of residential service and a measure of the mix of nonresidential services. These measures are described below.

Mix of services was indicated by the number of different certified mental health services that clients received in FY'96. There was a great deal of variance with respect to services received. Some 82 percent of the 113 clients received at least one certified mental health service, whereas 18 percent received no certified mental health service of any kind. Nine percent received one service, 21 percent received two services, 22 percent received three services, 17 percent received four services, and 8 percent received five services. The remaining 5 percent received from six to eight services.

The 113 RMIs in the sample received an average of 2.6 services. When the mean is computed for just those clients receiving one or more services, the average is 3.2 services. Of those who received services, the most commonly reported service was case management; this was followed by "medication/somatic," which refers mainly to drug treatment and monitoring.

Intensity of residential services was measured in terms of number of days spent in a variety of residential programs, excluding inpatient residence in a psychiatric hospital. The average number of residential days in FY'96 for the RMIs was 54.

Family Burden Variables. Family burden was measured in 1996 in terms of assistance in daily living (Care; see Chapter 3), supervision of behavioral problems (Control; see Chapter 4), and financial expenditures (Financial; see Chapter 5). Each of the measures focused on objective burden, rather than subjective burden.

Other Variables. Although not included explicitly in the theoretical model, the equation includes RMI sex (1 = being female) and the

Table 11.3
Predicting Family Member Evaluations (N = 113)

Variable	Coefficient	Beta	Probability
RMI is female	.515	.237	.010
FM is adult child	-.422	-.157	.087
FM worried more	-.329	-.151	.081
Residential treatment (days)	-.001	-.151	.081
Service index	.129	.212	.030
1996 CARE (frequency)	.545	.360	.000
1996 CONTROL (frequency)	-.582	-.223	.020
1996 FINANCIAL	-.696	-.108	NS
Constant	2.33	-	.000

Note: Adjusted R^2 = .199

family role of adult child (1 = adult child) as control variables because they account for significant variance in family member satisfaction with professionals, services, and systems.

MultiVariate Findings

We used mulitiple regression to estimate the net effects of each of the variables in the model in predicting family satisfaction. Because the purpose of this analysis is exploratory, and the degrees of freedom are limited by the small number of cases, we report as statistically significant those results that meet the .10 criterion. The results are shown in Table 11.3.

As shown, family members tended to express more satisfaction if the RMI is female, and less satisfaction if the RMI is male, perhaps reflecting more compliance with treatment regimens by female RMIs. In addition, adult children tend to be more critical of professionals, services, and systems than other family members. This may reflect both the ambivalence felt by many adult children about caregiving for a parent with mental illness, and their lesser involvement in the system of care (see Chapter 10, Table 10.2). Evidently, less involvement does not ensure positive evaluations.

As hypothesized, deteriorating client functioning, measured by increased worry by FMs from 1995 to 1996, is associated with more negative evaluations of professionals, services, and systems. Also as hypothesized, the effect of mix of RMI services received in FY'96 on FM satisfaction in 1996 is positive; the greater the number of different types of certified mental health services RMIs received, the more satisfied were the FMs. However, the intensity of residential services was not significantly related to family satisfaction; and contrary to what was predicted suggests that as residential treatment days go up, FM satisfaction goes down. Thus, family members seem to be impressed with nonresidential mental health services, but underimpressed with community residential services.

The family burden results are complex. The more Care family members provided to their RMIs in activities of daily living, the more favorably they evaluated mental health professionals, services, and systems. In contrast, the more Control exerted by FMs over behavioral problems, the more critical their evaluations. A third dimension of family burden, Financial Expenditures, is also associated with more negative evaluations, but not significantly so.

DISCUSSION

When care is given freely, it probably does not result in resentment directed toward the formal system of care. In contrast, control is rarely given out of desire, and economic costs often engender ambivalence. Family members seem quite satisfied when the RMI is receiving a mix of services and his or her functioning has not deteriorated. The relationship of economic costs to family member evaluations of professionals, services, and systems appears to be affected by cross-pressures, with some FMs blaming the system for not providing more financial support, whereas others perceive at least some family expenditures on behalf of the RMI as appropriate and desired.

The tendency of family members to complain more about residential services, regardless of how their RMI is functioning, is hardly new. When family members are interviewed, they often complain about the quality of the neighborhoods where their relatives with mental illness live, citing drug problems, danger, and dirtiness. Parents in more affluent circumstances are particularly distressed by the need to choose between providing more comfortable surroundings for their sons and daughters and the need to encourage independence.

Relations between family members and professionals, both treatment providers and state mental health authorities, are changing. Professionals are recognizing the family's role in treatment and inviting them into treatment planning more than ever before. This does not mean that some family experiences with professionals are not frustrating, but at least the change is positive. By the same token, state mental health authorities appear to be taking family members more seriously than ever before, and inviting their input in system building and evaluation.

Unfortunately, we have yet to see family member evaluations included routinely in ongoing efforts to monitor the effectiveness of mental health services and programs (Schene, Tessler, and Gamache 1994). It is our hope that by introducing a new set of measures and illustrating how they can be used, we will have contributed in some modest way to the goal of including family response as one component, among others, in any systematic evaluation of mental health professionals, services, and systems.

Chapter 12

What Did Family Members Know about Mental Health Insurance Coverage?

During the 1990s, mental health insurance "parity" became an important issue for persons with serious mental illness, their family members, providers of mental health services, and state and federal legislators (Brodey et al. 1995; NAMI 1997). Many states introduced or planned to introduce legislation requiring that insurance companies provide "parity" for mental health problems in which the coverage would be equivalent to the benefits provided for physical health problems (Brodey et al. 1995). The passage of the federal Mental Health Parity Act in 1996 was an important first step toward achieving equality of coverage.

Discussions of parity brought to the forefront questions of the interrelationships of mental illness, insurance coverage, and work disincentives. Results from one study provided some evidence that "disabled persons [disabilities were not defined] who cannot immediately go from being unemployed to working full-time, or, who are only capable of part-time work, are likely to have a significant insurance-related work disincentive" (Burns, Batavia, and Dejong 1994, 57). Another group of researchers traced the pathways to SSI and SSDI disability income for persons with severe and persistent psychiatric disorders, and concluded that "[t]he dichotomous condition of being either on or off the benefit rolls [SSI and SSDI], with no feasible or understandable middle ground, is a widely recognized obstacle to a more reasonable policy" (Estroff et al. 1997, 524). As we contemplate future mental health policies under managed care, including those designed to encourage less reliance on publicly funded services, it is important to understand past trajectories that have led people with serious mental illness to rely almost exclusively on the public sector. In fostering such understanding, family members may serve as valuable informants.

There has long been the assumption that many persons currently receiving mental health services in the public sector previously had private insurance benefits that included some degree of mental health coverage. According to this set of beliefs, privately insured psychiatric benefits were lost when the person with mental illness turned 19 years of age and was no longer covered by a parent's policy, was unable to find or keep a job that included benefits, or for other reasons became ineligible for private health insurance. As Michael Faenza, president and chief executive officer of the National Mental Health Association, stated, "When people are denied mental health coverage under private insurance, their treatment needs do not vanish. The costs are merely shifted onto the very strained and often fragmented public sector systems" (1996). But the assumption that patients now in the public sector of care could be found previously in the private insurance sector has not been well documented.

In this chapter we present results from a special module included in the 1997 family member interview protocol. These questions asked family members about their relatives' current and past mental health insurance coverage and, if applicable, how their relative came to lose private insurance that covered mental illness. Our goals included identifying the prevalence of past private coverage, as well as factors that may be associated with it, such as race, co-residence, and relationship to the person with mental illness. We also wanted to ask family members about their attitudes toward parity between psychiatric and general health insurance coverage.

METHODS AND RESULTS

This section presents results of family member reports of the mental health coverage of their relatives. The introduction to the series of insurance questions read as follows:

Many people currently believe that insurance coverage for mental health care should be equal to insurance coverage for physical health care, so that in the

Table 12.1
Family Member Knowledge of Insurance (N = 113)

FM Has Knowledge of . . .	Know	Don't Know
current Medicaid	105	8
current Medicare	95	18
other current mental health coverage	108	5
past mental health coverage (n = 100 FMs saying no current coverage)	92	8
one or more sources of any current or past mental health coverage	86	27
RMI without coverage for needed services before age 18	100	13
RMI without coverage for needed services after age 18	107	6

future people with mental illness will be more likely to have adequate mental health coverage as soon as they are diagnosed with mental health problems. To help us understand the problems with coverage that persons with mental illness may be experiencing now or have experienced in the past, we would like to ask you some questions about your relative's health insurance.

Family Member Knowledge of Mental Health Coverage

Since we were relying on family members as key informants, it was important to determine how knowledgeable family members were about their relative's mental health insurance coverage. We assumed that the clearest indicator of lack of knowledge would be the proportion responding "don't know" to pertinent questions. The results are shown in Table 12.1.

Fortunately, "don't knows" constituted only a small proportion of the pertinent responses. Out of 113 interviewed family members, 105 had knowledge of the RMI's Medicare status and 95 had knowledge of the RMI's Medicaid status. Of the 105 FMs who had knowledge about Medicaid coverage, 79 percent said their relatives had this type of coverage. Of the 95 FMs who knew about Medicare coverage, 43 percent said their relatives were covered in this way. Thus, a total of 85 percent of the RMIs were covered under either the Medicaid or Medicare program, according to their family members.

Table 12.1 shows that most FMs also knew whether their relative had currently, or had ever had, alternative sources of insurance coverage. Family members reported that only 13 percent of the RMIs currently had private mental health insurance coverage. Slightly more (17 percent) were reported to have had such coverage in the past. FMs also appeared to be knowledgeable about whether their relatives had ever been without coverage for needed services. Fourteen FMs reported that this occurred before age 18, and 22 FMs said this happened after age 18.

We assumed that *knowledge about coverage* would vary by family role. In fact, there were significant differences by family relationship with respect to knowledge about Medicaid and Medicare (f = 3.71; df = 5, 107; p < .01). With the exception of siblings, knowledge of Medicaid and/or Medicare followed the general pattern of family role obligations to provide care and support. Ninety-five percent of spouses, 90 percent of parents, 83 percent of adult children, and 71 percent of "other relatives" knew about such coverage. Siblings were least likely to know; some 47.4 percent *did not know* about Medicaid and/or Medicare coverage. Perhaps because of their employment in the public system of care, all three fictive kin knew about the consumer's Medicaid and/or Medicare coverage.

As might be expected, co-residence was also significantly associated with knowledge of Medicaid and/or Medicare coverage. Ninety-seven percent of co-resident FMs knew about such coverage compared with 75 percent of non-co-resident FMs (X^2 = 8.92, df = 1, p < .01).

Sources of Private Mental Health Coverage

The 13 family members who reported that their relatives had *current* mental health insurance coverage other than Medicaid or Medicare were asked to identify the source(s) of coverage. Precoded choices included: the FM's own insurance policy; a/another parent's policy; his/her spouse's policy; his/her own employment; veterans' benefits; private mental health insurance that the FM purchased just for the relative; private mental health insurance that the relative purchased for himself/herself; or some other source. The distribution of sources is shown in Table 12.2.

Surprisingly, the most frequently reported source was private mental health insurance that the relative purchased for himself/herself. Six FMs out of the 13 reported this source. The next most frequently

Table 12.2
Sources of Private Mental Health Insurance Coverage

Source of Mental Health Coverage Other than Medicaid or Medicare	Current Coverage* (n = 13)		Past Coverage* (n = 13)		Most Recent Past Coverage (n = 13)	
	n	%	n	%	n	%
FM's own insurance policy	1	7.7	5	38.5	2	15.4
a/another parent's policy	2	15.4	3	23.1	2	15.4
RMI's spouse's policy	1	7.7	5	41.7	4	30.8
RMI's own employment	4	30.8	3	23.1	2	15.4
Veteran's benefits	1	7.7	1	7.7	1	7.7
private mental health insurance purchased by FM	1	7.7	1	7.7	0	-
private mental health insurance purchased by RMI	6	46.2	1	7.7	1	7.7
other source	0	0.0	2	15.4	1	7.7

Notes: *Totals may add to more than 100 percent because FMs named more than one source of coverage. Percentages are calculated only for the RMIs who had current or past sources of coverage that the FM could name.

cited source was the RMI's own employment. Four FMs reported that this was currently a source of mental health insurance coverage.

Four (out of 13) family members said the coverage requires co-payments, but only one said there was a dollar limit to the amount of benefits that can be provided over their relative's lifetime.

The 17 FMs who reported that their RMI had mental health insurance coverage *in the past*, other than Medicaid and Medicare, were also asked to identify the source(s) of coverage. The distribution of *past* sources of coverage is shown in Table 12.2 for the 13 FMs who were able to identify one or more sources.

The most frequently reported past sources (not the most recent) were coverage under a noninterviewed spouse's policy (n=5) and an interviewed FM's own insurance policy (n=5, these included one spouse, three parents, and one other relative). The least reported *past* sources were veterans' benefits, private mental health insurance that the FM purchased just for the relative, and private mental health insurance that the RMI purchased for himself/herself.

When there had been more than one source of past coverage, family members were asked which was the most recent. As is also shown in Table 12.2, the distribution of the most recent sources of coverage indicate that a spouse's policy was the most often reported recent (but not current) coverage (n = 4). The next most frequent sources were the FM's own insurance (n = 2), another parent's policy (n = 2), and the RMI's own employment (n = 2). Three FMs reported the single sources of veterans' benefits or private mental health insurance purchased by the RMI. When asked how long it had been since their relatives had had the most recent coverage, two FMs said one to two years, one said three to four years, and ten said it was five or more years ago.

The 13 FMs who reported (and knew) a source of past coverage were asked if co-payments were required. Four family members said they were required and six said they were not. Three FMs did not know. When the 13 were asked if there were a dollar limit to the amount of benefits that could be provided over the relative's lifetime, two FMs said yes and six said no. The remaining five FMs did not know.

Losing and Not Having Mental Health Coverage

We also asked family members to tell us how their relatives lost their past mental health insurance. Family members mentioned the closing down of a local source of employment, divorce from a spouse whose policy provided coverage, the RMI turning 18 and being dropped from a parent's insurance plan, and the loss of the RMI's own employment.

We then asked if the relative ever had the opportunity to get mental health insurance coverage back after she or he lost it. Five FMs said "yes" and eight said "no." Of the five FMs who said there was an opportunity for the RMI to get the coverage back, four replied that the RMI did get the insurance back. Only one FM said that their relative had an opportunity but failed to get the insurance back. When asked to tell us why the opportunity had been lost, the family member did not know.

We asked all 113 FMs if there were ever a time that the relative needed mental health services but there was no insurance coverage to pay for them. Fourteen FMs said this happened before the age of 18, and 22 said this happened after the age of 18.

Patterns of Private Coverage

Having current or prior mental health coverage was significantly and negatively associated with currently having Medicaid coverage, but not with having current Medicare coverage. A history of *prior* coverage is significantly associated with current Medicare coverage, but not with *current* Medicaid coverage.

At the bivariate level, fewer years of RMI education is significantly associated with *currently* receiving Medicaid. There is also a tendency for lower education to be associated with current Medicare coverage, but the association is significant only at the p < .10 level. *Ever* having had prior mental health insurance coverage (other than Medicaid or Medicare) is significantly associated with race. A minority status is associated with having no prior coverage. But *past* coverage is not associated with family member reports of low household income for the three years 1994, 1995, and 1996. Nor is *past* coverage associated with client age, sex, or education.

A logistic regression was used to predict a dichotomous dependent variable set equal to 1 if the RMI *ever* (currently or in the past) had mental health coverage other than Medicaid or Medicare, and equal to 0 if he or she *never* had any other coverage according to FMs. Independent variables included RMI Race (1 = black, 0 = white); Poor Area (1 = the economically disadvantaged areas of the Trumbull County site in northeast Ohio [the Youngstown/Warren area] and southern Ohio/Appalachia [the Adams-Lawrence-Scioto County Board along the Ohio River] *compared with* 0 = northwest Ohio [the Four County Board area west of Toledo] and the Montgomery County site [mainly the city of Dayton in southwest Ohio]; Schizophrenia (1 = a diagnosis of schizophrenia and 0 = otherwise); Age (RMI age in years); Education (RMI education in years); and an interaction term labeled Poor Area *Diagnosis. RMI Sex (1= female, 0 = male) and RMI Age (in years) are included as control variables. The results of the logistic regression are shown in Table 12.3.

Inspection of the results indicates that there is a definable population whose life circumstances leave them little choice but to turn to the public sector for mental health care or to risk the consequences of not receiving professional help. Persons with mental illness who are members of a minority, who live in economically disadvantaged (as compared with more advantaged) areas, who have a diagnosis of schizophrenia, and who tend to have less formal education, are rela-

Table 12.3
Predicting Private Mental Health Insurance Coverage (N = 107)

Variable	Log Likelihood (Odds Ratio)	Logit Estimates (Coefficient)
Race	.171**	-1.76**
Poor Area	.254**	-1.37**
Schizophrenia	.260**	-1.35**
Interaction Poor Area* Diagnosis	10.7**	2.37**
Education	1.21*	.191*
Age	1.01	.011
Sex	.470	-.755

Notes: Pseudo R^2 = .1472; *p ≤.05; **p ≤.10

tively unlikely to have ever had mental health insurance coverage other than Medicaid or Medicare. Conversely, nonminority persons with mental illness who do not live in disadvantaged areas, who have a diagnosis other than schizophrenia, and who tend to have had more education, have a higher likelihood of currently having or having had private mental insurance coverage. These results are obtained controlling for the age and sex of the RMI.

The results also indicate an interaction effect, such that persons with diagnoses of schizophrenia who also live in economically disadvantaged areas are especially unlikely to have a history of private mental health insurance coverage. This pattern could arise from the early onset of schizophrenia, which, when it occurs, tends to preclude the normal adult route to private insurance through employment benefits. Alternatively, the relative poverty of their FMs may also have contributed to a trajectory that leads RMIs with schizophrenia, a particularly costly form of mental illness, to avoid the private sector of care from the onset of treatment.

Importance of Parity to Family Members

We concluded the insurance module by asking all 113 family members the following question about parity: How important do you think it is that legislation requires that mental health benefits be equal to general health benefits? Is it "extremely" (coded 5), "very" (coded 4), "somewhat" (coded 3), "a little" (coded 2), or "not at all" important (coded 1)? The mean score for the 112 FMs who answered this question is 4.81 (close to *extremely* important). No family member said it was *not at all* or *a little* important.

A one-way analysis of variance showed that there are significant differences (f = 4.69, df 5,106, p = .0007) among the various family roles. Unexpectedly, siblings attached the most importance to parity (mean = 5.0); followed by adult children (mean = 4.91); parents (4.88); other relatives (4.71); and fictive kin (4.67). Spouses scored the lowest (mean = 4.45). Unexpectedly, family members who live with their relative with mental illness scored significantly (f = 8.33, df 1,110, p = .0047) *lower* (mean = 4.65) compared with family members who do not live with their relative (mean = 4.89). There was also a tendency (f = 2.95, df 1,110, p = .089) for female family members to think parity was more important (mean = 4.85) than males did (mean = 4.67).

DISCUSSION

Many advocates have observed how the current structuring of health care insurance discriminates against persons with serious mental illness. The lifetime limits for reimbursement of costs are far more restrictive than in the general health sector, and exclusions associated with prior conditions tend to be even more severe. The passage of the federal Mental Health Parity Act of 1996 sought to correct some of the inequities that have existed between coverages for physical disorders and mental health problems.

Beginning in 1998, the legislation disallowed *group* health plans from providing $1 million in lifetime benefits with no annual cap for illnesses such as cancer, diabetes, and heart disease, when by contrast the mental health coverage includes a $10,000 limit for mental health care and a $5,000 annual cap (Faenza 1996; NAMI 1998). Although the new federal act seeks to correct inequities, the legislation is limited. Parity is mandated only if companies provide mental health benefits, and is a nonissue if mental health benefits are not provided in the first place. In addition, insurance companies may still impose arbitrary inpatient and outpatient limitations, and insurers may charge higher co-payments and deductibles for mental health services, including psychiatric hospitalization.

With discriminatory practices such as these, adults with serious and persistent psychiatric disorders have found themselves faced with a dilemma. As *adults* with serious mental illnesses, they are not entitled to coverage under a parental policy. At the same time, they may be unable to function in the workplace, either by getting or keeping jobs. Without private insurance to pay for needed mental health services, including psychiatric medications critical to functioning in the community, they must be formally certified as eligible for public sector services. If they then find jobs that do not provide mental health insurance benefits, or that provide only limited benefits, they lose access to the services that enable them to work in the first place. Thus, the current structure of mental health insurance coverage includes economic disincentives to get well and to leave the public sector even though it is not necessarily the sector of choice for either clients or their families.

Although there was some uncertainty about sources of coverage, including who was the payee, family members in general claimed more knowledge than ignorance about their relative's mental health insurance coverage. Based on FM reports, it appears fair to conclude that relatively few of their RMIs currently have, or have ever had, alternative sources of insurance coverage. For the vast majority who depend totally on the public sector for their care, parity between privately insured health and mental health care is really a nonissue. Without universal health care available as an entitlement to all who are in need, the combination of a disabling mental illness and economic disadvantage will continue to drive most of these patients and their families into the public sector.

PART IV

Implications

Chapter 13

Dilemmas of Kinship

As has been documented throughout this book, the family experience with mental illness is fraught with dilemmas of kinship, including whether or not to provide informal care, whether to share a home or to encourage independent living, and whether or not to get involved in treatment planning. In this concluding chapter, we discuss research findings on the family experience in the context of dilemmas such as these.

In Chapter 1, we stated that although it is difficult to estimate precisely the number of family members in the United States who have relatives with serious mental illness, it is likely that they number at least a million and a half. Thus, if these family members (many of whom provide informal care) are to receive help from the formal system of care, there is a clear need for programs that are based on research on their experiences. Accordingly, in this chapter, we will trace some of the implications of research on the family experience for family members who are affected by a relative's mental illness. We will also highlight implications for mental health professionals who seek to promote community living, and policy makers who are responsible for designing and evaluating programs.

One of the initial dilemmas family members face is how to label or conceptualize the problem. A diagnosed mental disorder may not always be defined as an illness by family members. The relatives' behaviors may be attributed to a personality defect, a moral failing, a supernatural basis, a lack of motivation, a physical injury, or seen as the result of substance abuse rather than as the symptoms of a biological illness. The more that troublesome and burdensome behaviors are seen as under the relative's control, the less likely family members will be to accept behaviors as symptoms of an illness.

Because mental illnesses may result in bewildering conduct, family members may be faced with a range of behaviors that require caregiving decisions that go beyond the realm of everyday routine events. Family members have reported that much of their distress is indeed linked to behavior management issues. In response to behaviors that are bizarre or disruptive, relatives of persons with mental illness may use rational arguments, emotional pleas, threats, or appeals to third parties such as social workers or, in extreme cases, the police.

It is only natural for family members to be distressed by the stigma that is directed toward their relative with mental illness, and toward themselves as family members. Likewise, it is only natural for them to be upset by disruptive behaviors such as substance abuse or noncompliance with prescribed medications, and by the one-sidedness of the relationship with the relative with mental illness. If caregiving is to continue over the long term, it is crucial that family members experience positive feelings toward their relative with mental illness. The challenge for professionals is to support families so that the kinship bond does not unravel.

Thus, a fundamental dilemma for family members, and for professionals who seek to help *them*, is how to sustain positive feelings in the face of stigma, frustration over problematic behaviors, and the perception that the relationship is unlikely to ever be fully reciprocal. Positive feelings tend to be easier to sustain if the family is part of a self-help group, if the relative with mental illness is receiving a variety of services from professionals, and if the relative is contributing in some way to the life of the family.

For some family members, *caring for* a relative with mental illness may bring special rewards, not the least of which is the knowledge that one is being helpful and that the relative is safe and secure. Other household family members who *care about* a relative with mental illness may also enjoy the person's company, and experience happiness as a result of their continuing relationship. Whether these positive feelings are greater, less than, or about equal in measure to negative feelings that are also part of the family experience will vary greatly both among and within families and households.

IMPROVING FAMILY OUTCOMES

Most readers are familiar with the concept of *patient outcome*, which refers to the prognosis for the patient, but are less familiar with the concept of *family outcome*, which is indicated by how well (or poorly) the family is able to come to terms with the mental illness of one of its members. In promoting positive family outcomes, the goal is to minimize the disruptive impact of the illness on other family members at the same time that steps are taken to help the patient. Without some type of intervention, most families are at risk for such negative outcomes as reduced attention to other family members, constraints on leisure time activities, and, in the worst case scenario, rejection of (or by) the relative with mental illness (Tessler et al. 1992). The challenge, therefore, is how to help families avoid negative outcomes and make positive outcomes at least imaginable.

If policy makers want to have a positive impact on families, they need to do something that affects them more or less directly. One such approach is to design supportive services specifically for families. State mental health authorities in Massachusetts and New Jersey have experimented with programs that reach out to families by organizing support groups so that family members discover that they are not alone and can benefit from one another's experiences, mobile teams that reach out to families when the client experiences a crisis, and respite care so that family caregivers (like professionals) can have some *time off*. Although experiences with state sponsored family support programs have been encouraging, these programs have also proven to be very vulnerable to budget cuts (Benson et al. 1996).

Supporting families also involves fostering better communication with professionals. Recent research on family attitudes toward professionals indicates improvement on some issues but not on others (see Chapter 11). Although there is certainly room for improvement, relations between families and professionals have come a long way from the old days, when concerned family members were treated as guilty of causing the illness.

A second approach to improving family outcomes involves self-help activities initiated by and for family members leading to activities that influence the formal system of care. Certainly, the family movement has been one of the most important developments in this field, yet barriers to participation remain for low-income groups, including membership fees, lack of public transportation and child care, and nighttime work, which makes it difficult for persons holding two jobs to "make ends meet" to attend evening meetings.

Among the dilemmas facing the mental health system is how best to coordinate support services offered by family groups with services that are organized by professionals. These need not be viewed as competing models for receiving support. The formal system of care also has a responsibility to make its services attractive to family members, some of whom want to be involved in treatment planning but do not believe their opinions will be heeded. The issue is magnified when the family member belongs to a cultural minority and the system of care reflects mainstream values and practices. Fortunately, mental health service providers are beginning to recognize that treatment is more accessible for both patient and family when it mirrors cultural preferences. Future choices may include culturally specific treatment services that both patients and families believe are appropriate to their ethnic background (Wilma Townsend, personal communication).

A third approach to improving family outcomes lies in concerted efforts to improve the organization and financing of mental health services for primary consumers. Although the process is indirect, services that benefit the patient are also likely to benefit the family. Whatever reforms are initiated, it is clear that they will need to be accompanied by new or expanded services that support consumers in such areas as supported housing, crisis services, assertive case management, and vocational rehabilitation.

However, it is very difficult to change a system of care in ways that affect patient outcomes, much less family outcomes. Even the most ambitious of patient-oriented reforms tend to make no discernible difference in terms of family burden. Our own evaluation of the impact of the RWJ Foundation's Program on Chronic Mental Illness indicated that positive family outcomes were modest at best and limited to situations where the client was living with the family (Tessler and Gamache 1994). In analyses carried out specifically for this book, we did find that financial expenditures by family members declined significantly over the life of the program, perhaps reflecting its emphasis on independent housing options for clients (see Chapter 5).

Many observers, including those in the family movement, are concerned with how the introduction of managed care is affecting family members, financially and otherwise. We need to learn from research whether under managed care family members perceive changes in the availability of services, whether their attitudes toward the public system of care change, and whether the burden of family caregiving increases, decreases, or remains the same. The good news in this book is that family burden did not appear to be increasing as one state mental health system evolved toward managed care (see Chapter 10).

It would be a mistake to infer from the existence of family caregivers who have adjusted to their roles, even to the point that they experience caregiving as personally gratifying, that care in the community can be accomplished without some burden to family members. By the same token, it would be a mistake to infer that families can or should supplant community services in the formal system of care.

DIRECTIONS FOR FUTURE RESEARCH

There remain some gaps and needs for future research. Not all family outcomes, nor indeed all families, have been included in family burden research, as the following points reveal.

First, burden researchers have focused mainly on the burden on the family of origin, particularly on parents, while ignoring the client's family of procreation. The fact that the fertility rate among women with mental illness is approaching that of the general population underscores the need to pay more attention to the family of procreation, including the burden to family members of caring for minor children. Many social service agencies attempt to place children with relatives before considering alternative foster care arrangements. Yet for family members, caring for the minor children of parents with mental illness may result in high levels of stress. The consequences of this burden may be the removal of the child(ren) from the extended family and placement in foster care. These children have been referred to as "invisible" from the mental health services perspective.

Second, the burden of caring for a child with a serious emotional disturbance has been less studied than when the relative is an adult with mental illness. This is an important future area of study because the burden of caring for a child may be a significant factor affecting placement decisions, with major consequences for the child, the family, and society. There is also interest in measuring the burden on foster parents who are caring for a child with serious emotional disturbance.

Third, most of our knowledge of family burden comes from studies carried out in urban and suburban areas. But rural areas are unique in a variety of ways that are likely to affect the family experience. Rural areas may contain pockets of extreme poverty, families may be isolated from formal sources of care, and there is possibly more stigma associated with seeking psychiatric help. However, the rural family is also thought to be more inclusive and may be more accepting of the relative with mental illness. Thus, for example, kin with mental disorders may find a role in rural households that would be unusual in urban and suburban areas.

Fourth, most family burden studies have focused on the major mental illnesses, especially schizophrenia and the affective disorders. Little is known about the burden to families arising from other disorders including somatization, anxiety, obsessive-compulsive behavior, and eating and personality disorders. The connection between substance abuse disorders and family burden has also received little attention despite the growing evidence of co-morbidity among persons with severe mental illness.

Fifth, family burden researchers need to continue to examine positive as well as negative experiences. To focus solely on the negative is to ignore the reality of family life, including the accordion nature of the relationship between persons with mental illness and their family members (Stoneall 1983).

Sixth, researchers more or less agree about the dimensions that make up the family burden concept, but there is less agreement on the definition of burden and how best to measure it. As already noted, there now exist many burden instruments with much overlap but also with many differences. Although it is encouraging to see that the field is growing, this can end in a situation where there are too many instruments and none that is readily accepted as a standard measure. Perhaps the time has come for burden researchers to join and develop a few standard instruments for research and routine clinical use.

A final suggestion is to incorporate family outcome measures as an integral part of the evaluation of mental health programs. Family experiences are rarely taken into account but need to be as state mental health authorities (and many others, including those in the private sector) evaluate new as well as ongoing services. Among the issues that warrant inclusion in family member evaluations are accessibility, integration of service delivery systems, crisis response, involvement of a family member in the treatment plan, client choice among options, and adequacy of the system of care and services (see Chapter 11).

CONCLUSION

The persistence of many mental illnesses throughout the life course suggests that mental health practitioners need to be prepared to support family members over the long term. In so doing, they will also need to come to terms with the very real limitations of the public system of care under deinstitutionalization. Without the hospital as a long-term alternative, family members have had to deal with a decentralized system that is too frequently fragmented, difficult to access, and unresponsive, leaving the family as the safety net of last resort. Major changes are again under way in the organization, delivery, and financing of mental health services, but as noted throughout this book, they hold uncertain implications for family members.

In designing programs for the future, we need to be very clear about the goals of the program and who is the target population. Research on the family experience indicates that there is a considerable diversity of experiences based on the characteristics of the family member and the relative with mental illness. In addition, the multidimensionality of burden further complicates the challenge of program design and evaluation. No single program or intervention will be suitable for all family circumstances. Nor is it reasonable to expect a single program to address all dimensions of the family experience, including grief, financial hardship, housing and other basic needs, and socially disruptive behavior, while also providing real opportunities for the relative with mental illness to be self-sufficient.

Research has shown that families pass through different stages in coming to terms with the mental illness of a close relative, but these are only rarely considered in designing programs (Tessler, Killian, and Gubman 1987). A program that meets the needs of families who have just been faced with the mental illness of a relative will not necessarily meet the needs of families who have 20 years of experience and considerable expertise derived from that experience. Nor should it be assumed that programs that meet the important needs of parents will also meet the important needs of spouses, children, siblings, and significant others. As we have shown throughout this book, the felt obligations and responsibilities of family members vary greatly by family role.

To conclude on a more optimistic note, the terrain for families is much better than it was even 20 years ago. Family blaming is on the wane and relations with professionals are improving. Alternatives for organized support, both formal and informal, are greater than ever before. Families now have a collective voice when it comes to proposed system changes such as managed care and legislative initiatives such as parity. But many goals remain to be accomplished if concerned family members and their loved ones with mental illness are to receive the supportive services they deserve.

Bibliography

Aiken, L., S. Somers, and M. Cohen. 1986. "Private Foundations in Health Affairs: A Case Study of a National Initiative for the Chronically Mentally Ill." *American Psychologist* 41: 1290–1295.

American Orthopsychiatric Association. 1987. "A Tribute to Family Members: Advocates for Social Change." Presented at a Special Session of the American Orthopsychiatric Association, Washington, DC. March 28, 1987.

Ascher-Svanum, H., and T. S. Sobel. 1989. "Caregivers of Mentally Ill Adults: A Woman's Agenda." *Hospital and Community Psychiatry* 40: 843–845.

Baldessarini, R. J. 1994. "Long-Term Treatment with Antipsychotic & Mood-Altering Agents." Presented at the University of Massachusetts Symposium on Long-Term Psychiatric Care, April, 1994.

Benson, P. R., G. A. Fisher, A. Diana, L. Simon, G. Gamache, R. C. Tessler, and M. McDermeit. 1996. "A State Network of Family Support Services: The Massachusetts Family Support Demonstration Project." *Evaluation and Program Planning* 19(1): 27–39.

Bernheim, K. F. 1989. "Psychologists and Families of the Severely Mentally Ill: The Role of Family Consultation." *American Psychologist* 44: 561–564.

Bernheim, K. F., and T. Switalski. 1988. "Mental Health Staff and Patients' Relatives: How They View Each Other." *Hospital and Community Psychiatry* 39: 63–68.

Biegel, D., and associates. 1992. "The Role of Race in Family Caregiving with Persons with Mental Illness: Burden, Support Systems and Use of Self-Help." Executive Summary of Final Report to the Office of Program Evaluation and Research, Ohio Department of Mental Health.

Biegel, D. E., S. E. Milligan, P. L. Putnam, and L. Song. 1994. "Predictors of Burden among Lower Socioeconomic Status Caregivers of Persons With Chronic Mental Illness." *Community Mental Health Journal* 30(5): 473–494.

Biegel, D. E., E. Sales, and R. Schulz. 1991. *Family Caregiving in Chronic Illness: Alzheimer's Disease, Cancer, Heart Disease, Mental Illness and Stroke*. Newbury Park, CA: Sage Publications.

Biegel, D. E., L. Song, and S. E. Milligan. 1995. "A Comparative Analysis of Family Caregivers' Perceived Relationships With Mental Health Professionals." *Psychiatric Services* 46(5): 477–482.

Brodey, B. B., M. P. Quirk, C. S. Dagadakis, T. D. Koepsell, and G. J. Tucker. 1995. "Mental Health Benefit Design: Striving to Achieve Parity in Washington State." *Psychiatric Services* 46(11): 1123–1125.

Bulger, M. W., A. Wandersman, and C. R. Goldman. 1993. "Burdens and Gratifications of Caregiving: Appraisal of Parental Care of Adults with Schizophrenia." *American Journal of Orthopsychiatry* 63: 255–265.

Burns, T. J., A. I. Batavia, and G. Dejong. 1994. "The Health Insurance Work Disincentive for Persons with Disabilities." In *Research in the Sociology of Health Care, Volume 11*, edited by R. Weitz and J. J. Kronenfeld, 57–68. Greenwich, CT: JAI Press.

Carpentier, N., A. Lesage, J. Goulet, P. Lalonde, and M. Renaud. 1992. "Burden of Care of Families Not Living with Young Schizophrenic Relatives." *Hospital and Community Psychiatry* 43(1): 38–43.

Clark, R. E. 1994. "Family Costs Associated with Severe Mental Illness and Substance Use." *Hospital and Community Psychiatry* 45(8): 808–813.

Clark, R. E., and R. E. Drake. 1994. "Expenditures of Time and Money by Families of People with Severe Mental Illness and Substance Use Disorders." *Community Mental Health Journal* 30: 145–163.

Clausen, J. A., and M. R. Yarrow. 1955. "Introduction: Mental Illness and the Family." *Journal of Social Issues* XI(4): 3–5.

Cockerham, W. C. 1992. *Sociology of Mental Disorder*. 3rd ed. Englewood Cliffs, NJ: Prentice Hall.

Cohen, M. D., and S. Sommers. 1990. "Supported Housing: Insights from the Robert Wood Johnson Foundation Program on Chronic Mental Illness." *Psychosocial Rehabilitation Journal* 13(4): 43–50.

Cook, J. A. 1988. "Who 'Mothers' the Chronically Mentally Ill?" *Family Relations* 37: 42–49.

Cook, J., and B. Cohler. 1986. "Reciprocal Socialization and the Care of

Offspring with Cancer and with Schizophrenia." In *Life-Span Developmental Psychology: Intergenerational Relations*, edited by N. Datan, A. L. Greene, H. W. Reese. Mahwah, NJ: Lawrence Erlbaum Associates.

Cook, J. A., H. P. Lefley, S. A. Pickett, and B. J. Cohler. 1994. "Age and Family Burden among Parents of Offspring with Severe Mental Illness." *American Journal of Orthopsychiatry* 64(3): 435–447.

Coulton, C. J., V. Fitch, and T. P. Holland. 1985. "A Typology of Social Environments in Community Care Homes." *Hospital and Community Psychiatry* 36(4): 373–377.

Creer, C., E. Sturt, and T. Wykes. 1982. "The Role of Relatives." In *Psychological Medicine*, Monograph Supplement 2, *Long-Term Community Care: Experience in a London Borough*, edited by J. K. Wing, 29–55. London: Cambridge Press.

Crotty, P., and R. Kulys. 1986. "Are Schizophrenics a Burden to their Families? Significant Others' Views." *Health and Social Work* (summer): 173–188.

Derogatis, L. R., and P. A. Cleary. 1977. "Confirmation of the Dimensional Structure of the SCL-90: A Study in Construct Validation." *Journal of Clinical Psychology* 33: 981–989.

Downs, M. W., and J. C. Fox. 1993. "Social Environments of Adult Homes." *Community Mental Health Journal* 29(1): 15–23.

Elkind, D. 1994. *Ties That Stress: the New Family Imbalance*. Cambridge, MA: Harvard University Press.

Estroff, S. E. 1981. *Making It Crazy: An Ethnography of Psychiatric Clients in an American Community*. Berkeley, CA: University of California Press.

Estroff, S. E., D. B. Patrick, C. R. Zimmer, and W. S. Lachicotte, Jr. 1997. "Pathways to Disability Income among Persons with Severe, Persistent Psychiatric Disorders." *The Milbank Quarterly* 75(4): 495–540.

Estroff, S. E., C. Zimmer, W. S. Lachicotte, and J. Benoit. 1994. "The Influence of Social Networks and Social Support on Violence by Persons with Serious Mental Illness." *Hospital and Community Psychiatry* 45: 6669–6679.

Faenza, M. M. 1996. "Federal Mental Health Parity Law." *Focal Point*, vol. 10.

Farber, B. 1973. *Family & Kinship in Modern Society*. Illinois: Scott, Foresman and Company.

Fisher, G. 1989. "The Probable Effects of Family Support Program Services on Burden and Attitudes toward Mental Health Professionals." Unpublished manuscript. University of Massachusetts, Amherst: Social and Demographic Research Institute.

Fisher, G. A., P. R. Benson, and R. C. Tessler. 1990. "Family Response to Mental Illness: Developments since Deinstitutionalization." In *Re-*

search in Community and Mental Health, Volume 6, edited by J. R. Greenley, 203–236. Greenwich, CT: JAI Press.

Fisher, G. A., R. C. Tessler, R. W. Manderscheid, and I. B. Sommers. 1992. "Sheltering the Severely Mentally Ill in the Community: A Sequential Decision Model." In *Research in Community and Mental Health, Volume 7*, edited by J. R. Greenley and P. Leaf, 155–176. Greenwich, CT: JAI Press.

Fox, R. C. 1989. *The Sociology of Medicine: A Participant Observer's View*. Englewood Cliffs, NJ: Prentice Hall.

Francell, C. G., V. S. Conn, and D. P. Gray. 1988. "Families' Perceptions of Burden of Care for Chronic Mentally Ill Relatives." *Hospital and Community Psychiatry* 39: 1296–1300.

Franks, D. D. 1987. *Report on Economic Expenses of Families of the Chronically Mentally Ill*. Division of Biometry and Applied Sciences, NIMH.

Franks, D. D. 1990. "Economic Contribution of Families Caring for Persons with Severe and Persistent Mental Illness." *Administration and Policy in Mental Health* 18: 9–18.

Freeman, H. E., and O. G. Simmons. 1963. *The Mental Patient Comes Home*. New York: John Wiley.

Gallagher, S., and D. Mechanic. 1993. "Living with the Mentally Ill: Health Outcomes for Non-Mentally Ill Household Members." Paper presented at the 88th Annual Meeting of the American Sociological Association, Miami, FL.

Gamache, G., and R. Tessler. 1995. "Mental Illness and the Family Household." Paper presented at the 72nd Annual Meeting of the American Orthopsychiatric Association, Chicago, IL.

Gamache, G., and R. Tessler. 1998. "Evaluating Family Experiences with Clients and Services in Ohio," Final Report to the Office of Program Evaluation and Research, Ohio Department of Mental Health, Columbus, Ohio.

Gamache, G., R. Tessler, and J. Nicholson. 1995. "Child Care as a Neglected Dimension of Family Burden. Research." In *Research in Community and Mental Health, Volume 8*, edited by J. R. Greenley. Greenwich, CT: JAI Press.

Goffman, E. 1971. *Relations in Public*. New York: Basic Books.

Goldman, H. H. 1982. "Mental Illness and Family Burden: A Public Health Perspective." *Hospital and Community Psychiatry* 33(7): 557–559.

Goldman, H. H. et al. 1994. "Evaluating the Robert Wood Johnson Foundation Program on Chronic Mental Illness." *The Milbank Quarterly* 72(1): 37–47.

Goldman, H. H., A. Lehman, J. Morrissey, S. Newman, R. Frank, and D. Steinwachs. 1990. "Design for the National Evaluation of the Robert

Wood Johnson Foundation Program on Chronic Mental Illness." *Hospital and Community Psychiatry* 41: 1217–1221.

Goldman, H. H., J. P. Morrissey, and M. S. Ridgely. 1994. "Evaluating the Robert Wood Johnson Foundation Program on Chronic Mental Illness." *The Milbank Quarterly* 72(1): 37–47.

Goode, W. J. 1960. "A Theory of Role Strain." *American Sociological Review* 25: 488–496.

Graham, R. W. 1983. "Adult Day Care: How Families of the Dementia Patient Respond." *Journal of Gerontological Nursing* 15: 27–31.

Greenberg, J. S., J. R. Greenley, and P. Benedict. 1994. "Contributions of Persons with Serious Mental Illness to Their Families." *Hospital and Community Psychiatry* 45: 475–480.

Greenberg, J. S., J. R. Greenley, D. McKee, R. Brown, and C. Griffin-Francell. 1993. "Mothers Caring for an Adult Child with Schizophrenia: The Effects of Subjective Burden on Maternal Health." *Family Relations* 42: 205–211.

Greenberg, J. S., M. M. Steltzer, and J. R. Greenley. 1993. "Aging Parents of Adults with Disabilities: The Gratifications and Frustrations of Later-life Caregiving." *The Gerontologist* 33(4): 542–550.

Greenberg, M. S. and S. P. Shapiro. 1971. "Indebtedness: An Aversive Aspect of Asking for and Receiving Help." *Sociometry* 34: 290–301.

Greenley, J. R. 1986. "Social Control and Expressed Emotion." *Journal of Mental and Nervous Disease* 174: 24–30.

Grella, C. E., and O. Grusky. 1989. "Families of the Seriously Mentally Ill and Their Satisfaction with Services." *Hospital and Community Psychiatry* 40: 831–835.

Guarnaccia, P. 1994. "Ethnicity, Social Status, and Families' Experiences of Caring for a Mentally Ill Family Member." Institute for Health, Health Care Policy and Aging Research, Rutgers University.

Gubman, G. D., and R. C. Tessler. 1987. "The Impact of Mental Illness on Families: Concepts and Priorities." *Journal of Family Issues* 8: 226–245.

Harding, C. M., G. W. Brooks, T. Ashikaga, J. S. Strauss, and A. Breier. 1987. "The Vermont Longitudinal Study of Persons with Severe Mental Illness, II: Long-Term Outcome of Subjects Who Retrospectively Met DSM-III Criteria for Schizophrenia." *American Journal of Psychiatry* 144(6): 727–735.

Hatfield, A. B. 1978. "Psychological Costs of Schizophrenia to the Family." *Social Work* (September): 355–359.

Hatfield, A. B. 1979. "The Family as Partner in the Treatment of Mental Illness." *Hospital and Community Psychiatry* 30: 338–340.

Hatfield, A. B. 1983. "What Families Want of Family Therapists." In *Family*

Therapy in Schizophrenia, edited by W. R. McFarlane, 41–65. New York: Guilford Press.

Hatfield, A. B. 1987. "Families as Caregivers: A Historical Perspective." In *Families of the Mentally Ill: Coping and Adaptation*, edited by A. B. Hatfield and H. P. Lefley, 3–29. New York: Guilford Press.

Hatfield, A. B. 1994. "Education Programs for Families." Remarks presented at the Knowledge Exchange Workshop for Research on Families of Persons with Severe and Persistent Mental Illness, Reston, VA.

Hatfield, A. B., E. Farrell, and S. Starr. 1984. "The Family's Perspective on the Homeless." In *The Homeless Mentally Ill: A Task Force Report of the American Psychiatric Association*, edited by H. R. Lamb. Washington, DC: American Psychiatric Press

Haug, M. R. 1994. "Elderly Patients, Caregivers, and Physicians: Theory and Research on Health Care Triads." *Journal of Health and Social Behavior* 35: 1–12.

Hiday, V. A. 1995. "The Social Context of Mental Illness and Violence." *Journal of Health and Social Behavior* 36(2): 122–137.

Hoenig, J., and M. W. Hamilton. 1966. "The Schizophrenic Patient in the Community and his Effect on the Household." *International Journal of Psychiatry* 12: 165–176.

Hoge, M. A., L. Davidson, E. E. H. Griffith, W. H. Sledge, and R. A. Howenstine. 1994. "Defining Managed Care in Public-Sector Psychiatry." *Hospital and Community Psychiatry* 45(11): 1085–1089.

Holden, D., and P. Lewine. 1982. "How Families Evaluate Mental Health Professionals." *Schizophrenia Bulletin* 8: 626–633.

Horwitz, A., R. Tessler, G. Fisher, and G. Gamache. 1992. "The Role of Adult Siblings in Providing Social Support to the Severely Mentally Ill." *Journal of Marriage and the Family* 54 (February): 233–241.

Horwitz, A. V., and S. C. Reinhard. 1995. "Ethnic Differences in Caregiving Duties and Burdens Among Parents and Siblings of Persons with Severe Mental Illness." *Journal of Health and Social Behavior* 36: 138–150.

Horwitz, A. V., S. C. Reinhard, and S. Howell-White. 1996. "Caregiving as Reciprocal Exchange in Families With Seriously Mentally Ill Members." *Journal of Health and Social Behavior* 37(2): 149–162.

Johnson, D. L. 1990. "The Family's Experience of Living with Mental Illness." In *Families as Allies in Treatment of the Mentally Ill*, edited by H. P. Lefley and D. L. Johnson, 31–63. Washington, DC: American Psychiatric Press.

Kanter, J. H., R. Lamb, and C. Loeper. 1987. "Expressed Emotion in Families: A Critical Review." *Hospital and Community Psychiatry* 38(4): 374–380.

Kemp, D. R. 1994. *Biomedical Policy and Mental Health*. Westport, CT: Praeger Publishers.

Kreisman, D., and R. Blumenthal. 1995. "Emotional Overinvolvement: A Review and Examination of its Role in Expressed Emotion." In *Research in Community and Mental Health, Volume 8*, edited by J. R. Greenley, 3–39. Greenwich, CT: JAI Press.

Kreisman, D., R. Blumenthal, M. Borenstein, M. Woerner, J. Kane, A. Rifkin, and G. Reardon. 1988. "Family Attitudes and Patient Social Adjustment in a Longitudinal Study of Outpatient Schizophrenics Receiving Low-Dose Neuroleptic: The Family's View." *Psychiatry* 51: 3–13.

Kreisman, D. E., and V. D. Joy. 1974. "Family Response to the Mental Illness of a Relative: A Review of the Literature." *Schizophrenia Bulletin* 10: 34–57.

Kreisman, D. E., S. J. Simmens, and V. D. Joy. 1979. "Rejecting the Patient: Preliminary Validation of a Self-Report Scale." *Schizophrenia Bulletin* 5: 220–222.

Landy, D. 1977. "The Position of the Afflicted in Society." In *Culture, Disease, and Healing: Studies in Medical Anthropology*, edited by D. Landy. New York: Macmillan Publishing Co.

Leff, J., and C. Vaughn. 1985. *Expressed Emotion in Families: Its Significance for Mental Illness*. New York: Guilford Press.

Lefley, H. P. 1987a. "Aging Parents as Caregivers of Mentally Ill Adult Children: An Emerging Social Problem." *Hospital and Community Psychiatry* 38: 1063–1070.

Lefley, H. P. 1987b. "Behavioral Manifestations of Mental Illness." In *Families of the Mentally Ill: Coping and Adaptation*, edited by A. B. Hatfield and H. P. Lefley, 107–127. New York: Guilford Press.

Lefley, H. P. 1989. "Family Burden and Family Stigma in Major Mental Illness." *American Psychologist* 44(3): 556–560.

Lefley, H. P. 1996. *Family Caregiving in Mental Illness*. Thousand Oaks, CA: Sage.

Lefley, H. P., E. M. Nuehring, and E. W. Bestman. 1992. "Homelessness and Mental Illness: A Transcultural Family Perspective." In *Treating the Homeless Mentally Ill*, edited by H. R. Lamb, L. L. Bachrach, and F. I. Kass. Washington, DC: American Psychiatric Association.

Lehman, A. F., L. T. Postrado, D. Roth, S. W. McNary, and H. H. Goldman. 1994. "Continuity of Care and Client Outcomes in the Robert Wood Johnson Foundation Program on Chronic Mental Illness." *The Milbank Quarterly* 72(1): 105–122.

Lehman, A. F., N. C. Ward, and L. S. Linn. 1982. "Chronic Mental Patients: The Quality of Life." *American Journal of Psychiatry* 139(10): 1271–1276.

Mapp, S. 1994 "Looking Out for the Mother's Helper." *Community Care* 2–8 (June): 22–23.

Maurin, J. T., and C. B. Boyd. 1990. "Burden of Mental Illness on the Family: A Critical Review." *Archives of Psychiatric Nursing* 4: 99–107.

Mechanic, D. 1994. "Establishing Mental Health Priorities." *The Milbank Quarterly* 72(3): 501–514.

Mechanic, D. 1999. *Mental Health and Social Policy: The Emergence of Managed Care.* 4th Edition. Boston, MA: Allyn and Bacon.

Medvane, L. J., and D. H. Krauss. 1989. "Causal Attributions and Parent-Child Relationships in a Self-Help Group for Families of the Mentally Ill." *Journal of Applied Social Psychology* 19: 1413–1430.

Miller, F., J. Dworkin, M. Ward, and D. Barone. 1990. "A Preliminary Study of Unresolved Grief in Families of Seriously Mentally Ill Patients." *Hospital and Community Psychiatry* 41(12): 1321–1325.

Minkler, M., and K. M. Roe. 1993. *Grandmothers as Caregivers: Raising Children of the Crack Cocaine Epidemic.* Newbury Park: Sage Publications.

Milstein, G., P. Guarnaccia, and E. Midlarsky. 1995. "Ethnic Differences in the Interpretation of Mental Illness." In *Research in Community and Mental Health, Volume 8,* edited by J. R. Greenley, 155–178. Greenwich, CT: JAI Press.

NAMI: National Alliance for the Mentally Ill. 1997. "Nearly 30 States Going for Parity This Year." *Spotlight, The Quarterly NAMI Campaign Review* 1(2): 2.

NAMI: National Alliance for the Mentally Ill. 1999. "The Mental Health Parity Act of 1996." Available via http://www.nami.org/update/parity96.html, September 16, 1999.

National Depressive and Manic-Depressive Association. 1993. Informational Bulletin of the National DMDA. Chicago: Author.

Newman, S. J. 1992. *The Severely Mentally Ill Homeless: Housing Needs and Housing Policy.* The Johns Hopkins University Institute for Policy Studies, Occasional Paper No. 12.

Newman, S. J., S. J. Rescchovsky, K. Kaneda, and A. M. Hendrick. 1994. "The Effects of Independent Living on Persons with Chronic Mental Illness: an Assessment of the Section 8 Certificate Program." *The Milbank Quarterly* 72(1): 171–198.

Nicholson, J., J. L. Geller, W. H. Fisher, and G. L. Dion. 1993. "State Policies and Programs That Address the Needs of Mentally Ill Mothers in the Public Sector." *Hospital and Community Psychiatry* 44(5): 484–489.

Norton, S., A. Wandersman, and C. R. Goldman. 1993. "Perceived Costs and Benefits of Membership in a Self-Help Group: Comparisons of Members and Nonmembers of the Alliance for the Mentally Ill." *Community Mental Health Journal* 29(2): 143–160.

Parsons, T., and R. Fox. 1952. "Illness, Therapy and the Modern Urban American Family." *Journal of Social Issues* 8: 31–44.

Pasamanick, B., F. R. Scarpitti, and S. Dinitz. 1967. *Schizophrenics in the Community: An Experimental Study in the Prevention of Hospitalization.* New York: Appleton-Century-Crofts.

Pickett, S. A. 1995. "Diversity in Family Experiences: Research on Ethnic Minority Families." Paper presented September 26–28 at NIMH-CMHS Workshop, St. Louis, MO.

Pickett, S. A., D. A. Vraniak, J. A. Cook, and B. J. Cohler. 1993. "Strength in Adversity: Blacks Bear Burden Better than Whites." *Professional Psychology: Research and Practice* 24(4): 460–467.

Platt, S., A. Weyman, S. Hirsch, et al. 1980. "The Social Behaviour Assessment Schedule [SBAS]: Rationale, Contents, Scoring, and Reliability of a New Interview Schedule." *Social Psychiatry* 15: 43–55.

Potasnik, H., and G. Nelson. 1984. "Stress and Social Support: The Burden Experienced by the Family of a Mentally Ill Person." *American Journal of Community Psychology* 12(5): 589–607.

Pulice, R. T., L. A. L. McCormick, and M. Dewees. 1995. "A Qualitative Approach to Assessing the Effects of System Change on Consumers, Families, and Providers." *Psychiatric Services* 46(6): 575–579.

Raymond, M. E., A. E. Slaby, and J. Lieb. 1975. "Familial Responses to Mental Illness." *Social Casework* 56: 492–498.

Reynolds, I., and J. E. Hoult. 1984. "The Relatives of the Mentally Ill: A Comparative Trial of Community-Oriented and Hospital-Oriented Psychiatric Care." *Journal of Nervous and Mental Disease* 172: 480–489.

Rogers, J., and P. Curtis. 1980. "The Concept and Measurement of Continuity in Primary Care." *American Journal of Public Health* 70(1): 122–127.

Rosenheck, R. A., J. Cramer, W. Xu, J. Thomas, W. Henderson, L. K. Frisman, C. Fye, and D. Charney, for the Department of Veterans Affairs Cooperative Study Group on Clozapine in Refractory Schizophrenia. 1997. "A Comparison of Clozapine and Haloperidol in Hospitalized Patients with Refractory Schizophrenia." *New England Journal of Medicine* 337: 809–815.

Rossi, A., and P. H. Rossi. 1990. *Of Human Bonding: Parent-Child Relations Across the Life Course.* New York: Aldine de Gruyter.

Rossi, P. H. 1989. *Down and Out in America: The Origins of Homelessness.* Chicago: University of Chicago Press.

Roth, D., T. F. Champney, J. Vercellini, B. G. Lauber, J. A. Clark, and G. Burns. 1994. "Services in Systems: Impact on Client Outcomes." In *New Research in Mental Health*, volume 11, edited by D. Roth. Ohio Department of Mental Health.

Scheff, T. J. 1984. *Being Mentally Ill: A Sociological Theory*. New York: Aldine.

Schene, A. H. 1990. "Objective and Subjective Dimensions of Family Burden: Toward an Integrative Framework for Research." *Social Psychiatry and Psychiatric Epidemiology* 25: 289–297.

Schene, A. H., R. C. Tessler, and G. M. Gamache. 1994. "Instruments Measuring Family or Caregiver Burden in Severe Mental Illness." *Social Psychiatry and Psychiatric Epidemiology* 29: 228–240.

Schene, A. H., R. C. Tessler, and G. M. Gamache. 1996 "Caregiving in Severe Mental Illness: Conceptualization and Measurement." In *Mental Health Service Evaluation*, edited by H. C. Knudson and G. Thornicroft, 296–316. Cambridge: Cambridge University Press.

Schulz, R., and D. E. Beigel. 1993. "Series Editors' Foreword." In *Grandmother as Caregivers: Raising Children of the Crack Cocaine Epidemic* by M. Minkler and K. M. Roe. Newbury Park: Sage Publications.

Shore, M., and M. Cohen. 1990. "The Robert Wood Johnson Foundation Program on Chronic Mental Illness: An Overview." *Hospital and Community Psychiatry* 41: 1212–1216.

Sommer, R. 1987. "Sons and Daughters of Parents in a Support Organization." *Psychiatric Quarterly* 58: 57–65.

Stack, C. B. 1974. *All Our Kin: Strategies for Survival in a Black Community*. New York: Harper & Row.

Steinwachs, D. 1979. "Measuring Provider Continuity in Ambulatory Care: An Assessment of Alternative Approaches." *Medical Care* 17: 551–565.

Stoneall, L. 1983. "Dilemmas of Support: Accordion Relations Between Families and the Deinstitutionalized Mentally Ill." *Journal of Family Issues* 4(4): 659–676.

Straznickas, K. A., D. E. McNiel, and R. L. Binder. 1993. "Violence toward Family Caregivers by Mentally Ill Relatives." *Hospital and Community Psychiatry* 44: 385–387.

Struening, E. L., A. Stueve, P. Vine, D. E. Kreisman, B. G. Link, and D. B. Herman. 1995. "Factors Associated with Grief and Depressive Symptoms in Caregivers of People with Serious Mental Illness." In *Research in Community and Mental Health, Volume 8*, edited by J. R. Greenley, 91–124. Greenwich, CT: JAI Press.

Susser, E. S., S. P. Lin, S. A. Conover, and E. L. Struening. 1991. "Childhood Antecedents of Homelessness in Psychiatric Patients." *American Journal of Psychiatry* 148: 1026–1030.

Sweet, J., L. Bumpass, and V. Call. 1988. "A National Survey of Families and Households, Codebook and Documentation: Survey Design and Content." Center for Demography and Ecology, University of Wisconsin-Madison.

Szasz, T. S. 1961. *The Myth of Mental Illness*. New York: Hoeber-Harper.

Tausig, M., J. Michello, and S. Subedi. 1999. *A Sociology of Mental Illness*. Upper Saddle River, NJ: Prentice Hall.

Tessler, R., and G. Gamache. 1994. "Continuity of Care, Residence, and Family Burden." *The Milbank Quarterly* 72(1): 149–169.

Tessler, R., and G. Gamache. 1995a. "The Family Burden Interview Schedule-Short Form (FBIS/SF)." In *Outcomes Assessment in Clinical Practice*, edited by L. Sederer and B. Dickey, 110–112 and 258–263. Baltimore: Williams and Wilkins.

Tessler, R., and G. Gamache. 1995b. *Toolkit for Evaluating Family Experiences with Severe Mental Illness*. Cambridge, MA: Human Services Research Institute.

Tessler, R., G. Gamache, and G. Fisher. 1991. "Patterns of Contact of Patients' Families With Mental Health Professionals and Attitudes Toward Professionals." *Hospital and Community Psychiatry* 42: 929–935.

Tessler, R., G. Gamache, D. Roth, and G. Burns. 1998. "Predicting Consumer Consent to Interview Primary Kinship Network Members." In *Research in Community and Mental Health, Volume 9*, edited by J. Morrissey. 251–266. Greenwich, CT: JAI Press.

Tessler, R., G. Gamache, P. H. Rossi, A. F. Lehman, and H. H. Goldman. 1992. "The Kindred Bonds Of Mentally Ill Homeless Persons." *New England Journal of Public Policy* 8(1): 265–280.

Tessler, R., and H. H. Goldman. 1982. *The Chronically Mentally Ill: Assessing Community Support Programs*. Cambridge, MA: Ballinger Publishing Company.

Tessler, R., L. M. Killian, and G. D. Gubman. 1987. "Stages in Family Response to Mental Illness: An Ideal Type." *Psychosocial Rehabilitation Journal* 10 (April): 3–16.

Tessler, R., G. Willis, and G. Gubman. 1986. "Defining and Measuring Continuty of Care." *Psychosocial Rehabilitation Journal* X(1): 27–38.

Thompson, E. H., and W. Doll. 1982. "The Burden of Families Coping with the Mentally Ill: An Invisible Crisis." *Family Relations* 31: 379–388.

Treudley, M. B. 1946. "Mental Illness and Family Routine." *Mental Hygiene* XXX(2): 177–249.

Wattie, B. J. A., and H. B. Kedward. 1985. "Gender Differences in Living Conditions Found among Male and Female Schizophrenic Patients on a Follow-Up Study." *The International Journal of Social Psychiatry* 31(3): 205–216.

Williams, P., W. A. Williams, R. Sommer, and B. Sommer. 1986. "A Survey of the California Alliance for the Mentally Ill." *Hospital and Community Psychiatry* 37: 253–256.

Yamamoto, N., and M. I. Wallhagen. 1997. "The Continuation of Family Caregiving in Japan." *Journal of Health and Social Behavior* 38(2): 164–176.

Index

About the Authors

RICHARD TESSLER is Professor of Sociology and Associate Director of the University of Massachusetts' Social and Demographic Research Institute. He is the senior author of *The Chronically Mentally Ill: Assessing Community Support Programs* and *West Meets East: Americans Adopt Chinese Children* (Bergin and Garvey, 1999).

GAIL GAMACHE is an Adjunct Assistant Professor and Senior Post-doctoral Research Associate at the University of Massachusetts. She has published numerous articles with Richard Tessler, and they recently co-authored, with Liming Liu, *West Meets East: Americans Adopt Chinese Children* (Bergin and Garvey, 1999).

ISBN 0-86569-251-3

HARDCOVER BAR CODE